Unpacking Your Learning Targets

This accessible resource assists teachers, instructional coaches, principals, and curricular leaders to adopt a simple, straightforward framework that allows educators to seamlessly align high quality learning targets with specific standards. Full of examples across grade levels and subjects, this useful book helps educators deepen their understanding of content and design more efficient lessons that will aid student learning and readiness. *Unpacking Your Learning Targets* is a guide into a deeper understanding of creating and designing learning targets that foster student learning and success for all.

Sean McWherter is Director of Restart Programs, Guilford County Schools, North Carolina, USA.

Other Eye On Education Books Available from Routledge
(www.routledge.com/eyeoneducation)

A Roadmap to PLC Success
Sean McWherter

Strategic Talent Leadership for Educators: A Practical Toolkit
Amy A. Holcombe

Becoming a Transformative Leader: A Guide to Creating Equitable Schools
Carolyn M. Shields

Bringing Innovative Practices to Your School: Lessons from International Schools
Jayson W. Richardson

Working with Students that Have Anxiety: Creative Connections and Practical Strategies
Beverley H. Johns, Donalyn Heise, Adrienne D. Hunter

Implicit Bias in Schools: A Practitioner's Guide
Gina Laura Gullo, Kelly Capatosto, and Cheryl Staats

Leadership in America's Best Urban Schools
Joseph F. Johnson, Jr, Cynthia L. Uline, and Lynne G. Perez

Leading Learning for ELL Students: Strategies for Success
Catherine Beck and Heidi Pace

Unpacking Your Learning Targets

Aligning Student Learning to Standards

Sean McWherter

Routledge
Taylor & Francis Group
NEW YORK AND LONDON

First published 2021
by Routledge
52 Vanderbilt Avenue, New York, NY 10017

and by Routledge
2 Park Square, Milton Park, Abingdon, Oxon, OX14 4RN

Routledge is an imprint of the Taylor & Francis Group, an informa business

© 2021 Taylor & Francis

The right of Sean McWherter to be identified as author of this work has been asserted by him in accordance with sections 77 and 78 of the Copyright, Designs and Patents Act 1988.

All rights reserved. No part of this book may be reprinted or reproduced or utilised in any form or by any electronic, mechanical, or other means, now known or hereafter invented, including photocopying and recording, or in any information storage or retrieval system, without permission in writing from the publishers.

Trademark notice: Product or corporate names may be trademarks or registered trademarks, and are used only for identification and explanation without intent to infringe.

Library of Congress Cataloging-in-Publication Data
Names: McWherter, Sean, author.
Title: Unpacking your learning targets : aligning student learning to standards / Sean McWherter.
Identifiers: LCCN 2020019624 (print) | LCCN 2020019625 (ebook) | ISBN 9780367460068 (hardback) | ISBN 9780367465940 (paperback) | ISBN 9781003029793 (ebook)
Subjects: LCSH: Education–Standards. | Academic achievement.
Classification: LCC LB3060.82 .M39 2020 (print) | LCC LB3060.82 (ebook) |
DDC 379.1/58–dc23
LC record available at https://lccn.loc.gov/2020019624
LC ebook record available at https://lccn.loc.gov/2020019625

ISBN: 978-0-367-46006-8 (hbk)
ISBN: 978-0-367-46594-0 (pbk)
ISBN: 978-1-003-02979-3 (ebk)

Typeset in Optima
by River Editorial Ltd, Devon, UK

Contents

Meet the Author   vi
Introduction   vii

1. **All Hands-on Deck**   1
2. **Standards**   8
3. **What Is a Learning Target?**   15
4. **Process**   24
5. **Standard Deconstruction**   28
6. **Word Wise**   37
7. **Cut the Fluff**   45
8. **Standard Reconstruction**   53
9. **With Higher Order Thinking in Mind**   61
10. **Write Learning Targets for the Standard**   75
11. **Assessing Your Learning Targets**   100
12. **Getting Started**   111

Meet the Author

Sean McWherter, Ed.D., has had the opportunity to directly serve disadvantaged students in kindergarten through 12th grade settings. He received his doctorate in Educational Leadership from Gardner-Webb University in 2012 and was a school-based administrator in both a high school and an elementary school prior to becoming a district-level administrator. He currently serves traditionally underperforming schools by training and supporting the implementation of innovative and best practices.

Dr. McWherter lives with his family in North Carolina.

Introduction

What does it mean to unpack a learning target? Unpacking learning targets refers to the framework that guides educators through the process of identifying and clearly communicating their learning objectives while ensuring that they fully align with both the curricular standards and the needs of the students.

I know educators already have a lot on their plate so let me be clear: I believe in working smarter not harder and I believe that the "extra" work we do should pay clear dividends in terms of student achievement. As such, I do not advocate doing senseless work without merit, and neither should you. We have an obligation to provide rigorous and equitable instruction to every student.

To the best of our ability we must use our time and resources to ensure that our students enter each new grade level with the appropriate knowledge and skills they need to be successful. This is where the importance of unpacking your learning targets is recognized.

Writing learning targets is a task that should only be completed after one is intimately familiar with the standards. This means that the logical timing for writing learning target(s) occurs while the corresponding standard(s) are being unpacked.

Even before the introduction of the Common Core there has been a constant evolution of instructional standards in the United States, this evolution has been driven by the need to define what knowledge and skills students should acquire in order to be successful after their traditional k-12 educational experience. In addition to defining knowledge and skills, it is equally important to specify what it means for students to learn. Teaching and learning are a complex relationship that requires teachers to adjust their pedagogy to match the diverse needs of their students.

The standards movement has historically reflected the belief that it is in the national interest to educate all students to their full potential (Lachat, 2004). In 1994, Congress passed legislation under the Elementary and Secondary Education Act (ESEA) to raise the bar of achievement for every American student. ESEA required states to replace their existing standards for poor and academically disadvantaged students with challenging standards for all students. The legislation also required states to develop new accountability systems to hold all students to the same performance standards (Riddle, 1996). In 2001 No Child Left Behind (NCLB) legislation added stronger accountability mandates and an increased emphasis on higher standards for all students (Lachat, 2004).

The push to increase the learning opportunities for all students was further promoted by the *Every Student Succeeds Act* (ESSA), passed in 2015. ESSA contains several provisions that advance equity and excellence for all students. ESSA requires states to design standards that develop and measure higher-order thinking skills for students, create multiple measures to assess school performance and progress, identify and address resource gaps for schools identified as needing intervention assistance, and utilize research-based approaches for school improvement (Cook-Harvey et al., 2016).

Since legislation first raised achievement expectations for all students, standards have been at the core of the federally mandated accountability systems directly aimed at improving the quality of teaching and learning. The belief is that educational opportunities for all students will improve if there are universal high-level standards for all students and standards-based assessments to hold districts, schools, and teachers accountable for the learning of their students (Lachat, 2004).

Every state in the United States, and every region in the United Kingdom has an established set of standards that are designated to guide the content taught at each grade level. The rationale for this is simple and logical: what a child learns in third grade should not differ from classroom to classroom or school to school. Otherwise, at the next grade level, students will have gaps in their exposure to required skills and curriculum and teachers will not have a clear starting point. Without mandated standards, it is impossible to have an equitable, effective educational system.

Introduction

The issue is not whether schools are better or worse than they used to be, but whether public schools are preparing all children to succeed in today's world (Lachat, 2004). The focus on standards in federal and state mandates has shifted the emphasis from "access for all", which we categorize as quality learning, to "high quality learning for all", which is a matter of equity (Lachat, 1999, 2004).

By clearly defining what all students need to learn, academic standards challenge educators to no longer accept low expectations for certain students and/or populations. There is a definitive connection between expectations for excellence and equity (Ravitch, 1995) that must be recognized if we are going to provide all students with the educational opportunities that they deserve. Requiring the development of problem solving and higher order thinking skills demands the improvement of equitable instructional approaches for all learners regardless of race, gender, or socioeconomic status. This vision of teaching and learning requires educators and the public to understand that high standards are as important in education as they are in the medical profession, in licensing pilots, or in international sports competitions such as the Olympics (Lachat, 2004).

However, no matter how well-crafted the standards are in their attempt to impart universal high-level learning outcomes, misinterpretations and/or inconsistent use at the school level can negate the advantages they should imbue. From an equity perspective, education standards will not improve student achievement by themselves. Standards need the support of high-quality curriculum, instruction, and assessments that align with and reflect high expectations for students (Lachat, 1999). Students need to have access to sustained high leverage instruction that leads to the development of higher order thinking and problem-solving skills (Stevens, 1996; Wolf & Reardon, 1993).

Why It Matters

If you believe that all students have the right to high quality rigorous instruction, then you believe in instructional equity. Equitable access to instruction is one of the most prevalent barriers that students face today. To break through this barrier, educators must change how we think about teaching standards and the way in which students are expected to learn

Introduction

those standards. "Standards hold the greatest hope for significantly improving student achievement" (Marzano, quoted in Schere, 2001). However, we have yet to universally enforce or properly implement standards (Marzano, 2001) and without systematic process of unpacking standards and learning targets, we will continue to face this barrier.

Ask yourself: What is the foundation that your lesson plans are built on? Is it a school or district template? Your years of teaching experience? Your pacing guide?

Although all these facets are important, the focal point or gravitas upon which your lesson plan is built must be the standard(s)-based learning outcome. It is the desired learning outcome(s) that shapes your learning target(s) which in turn shape your lesson(s). The lesson plan should not control the direction of the learning target. Allowing the lesson to shape the learning target is analogous to the tail wagging the dog.

Take a moment to consider ... if the learning target shapes the lesson plan(s), what determines the learning target?

(You are free to imagine your favorite game show music at this point)

If you responded with "standards" you are correct. If you didn't, that's okay.

Your content standards are the foundation for your learning targets just as your learning targets are the foundation for your lesson plans.

Therefore, the key to effectively developing learning targets that are fully aligned with the standards is to incorporate the process of writing learning targets into the same framework used for unpacking your standards. Unfortunately, many educators view the task of unpacking standards as cumbersome and unnecessary. Some also view it as completely detached from the process of creating learning targets. However, the process of unpacking standards directly lends itself to writing high quality learning targets that directly align to what should be taught in the classroom.

What Is This Book About?

The goal of this resource is to help educators to adopt and understand a logical and straightforward framework that will allow them to seamlessly integrate writing high quality learning targets within the process of unpacking standards.

By clearly illustrating the integration of writing learning targets within the unpacking framework, this resource will guide educators into a deeper understanding of the content so that they can create learning targets that guide their lessons and foster student learning and success.

This, in turn, will foster more efficient lessons that will aid student learning and readiness.

Who Is This Book For?

This book can serve as a resource for classroom teachers, instructional leaders (curriculum facilitators, lead teachers, coaches, mentors, etc.), school-based administrators, and central office personnel that support curriculum and instruction. If you are an educator whose primary focus is to deliver high quality lessons directly to students, or you are responsible for leading and/or supporting these amazing individuals, this resource is for you.

Still unsure if this is for you? If you answer "yes" to any of the questions below then you could potentially benefit from this resource.

> Do you want to...
> improve instructional alignment?
> increase student achievement?
> foster teacher mastery of their content?
> build a solid foundation to help increase the success of other instructional initiatives?

Organization and Chapter Overviews

Chapter 1 – All Hands on Deck

The opening chapter explains who should be involved in the process of unpacking your learning targets and why. It also provides rationale for why it is important to take the time to go through this process.

Chapter 2 – Standards

Many educators have concerns that they have too many standards and not enough time to teach them all, much less unpacking them all. I will

Introduction

share a process of identifying power standards and how it can be used to help manage one's workload.

Chapter 3 – What is a Learning Target

If written and used correctly, learning targets can play a critical role in both student achievement and teacher success. However, it is important that you know what learning targets are and are not and can explain/justify the importance of utilizing them in the classroom.

Chapter 4 – Process

This chapter will introduce the reader to the unpacking template that will guide the subsequent chapters.

Chapter 5 – Standard Deconstruction

Standard deconstruction is the first step in the unpacking process. This chapter will explain the importance of breaking down a standard to its essential words and phrases while also paying particular attention to the conjunctions and punctuation. Doing this allows educators to get to the central focus of the standard.

Chapter 6 – Word Wise

Even after a standard has been broken down to its essential words and phrases it is incorrect to assume that everyone defines and understands the words and terms the same way. Not only is it extremely important to make sure that the team is operating on the same page, but we must also ensure that their definition aligns with that of the authors of the standard. This chapter will explain why this often overlooked step is so important.

Chapter 7 – Cut the Fluff

This chapter will guide the reader through the process of reconstructing the essential words and phrases in a standard. The focus here remains specifically on what the students need to be able to do in a simple and easy to understand manner.

Chapter 8 – Standard Reconstruction

After completing the steps in the preceding chapters, readers should have the breadth/scope of understanding to reword the standard while still capturing its purpose and intent. This Chapter will guide the reader

Introduction

through that process and give them confidence to know and demonstrate their understanding of the standard.

Chapter 9 - With Higher Order Thinking in Mind

The union of cognitive thinking skills and learning targets is intended to help educators reap the benefits associated with the integration of higher order thinking skills while also providing them with a structured approach to scaffolding their learning targets in order to achieve the desired leaning outcome(s). Chapter 9 familiarizes readers with two of the most used cognitive thinking models, Bloom's Taxonomy and Webb's Depth of Knowledge, and establishes how critical their role is in one's instructional planning. Not only do higher order thinking skills allow students to more easily learn and understand concepts holistically, but they also promote reflective learning (Shukla & Dungsungnoen, 2016) and metacognition (Anderson & Krathwohl, 2001; Roberts & Erdos, 1993; Shukla & Dungsungnoen, 2016) and the integration of differentiated instruction (Anderson & Krathwohl, 2001). Incorporating higher order thinking skills into your learning targets will also assist you in appropriately scaffolding your lessons and research indicates that and the integration of scaffolded thinking routines can build student capacity and commitment toward thinking (Ritchhart, 2002, 2006).

Chapter 10 - Writing Learning Targets for the Standard

There is no better time to write the corresponding learning targets for a standard than when one is most familiar with the standard. This chapter represents the last phase in the unpacking process and will cover the two parts involved in this step. The first step is to create the overarching learning target for the standard. This frames the intent of the standard into something the students should be able to do, answer, demonstrate, or explain at the end of a series of lessons. The second step is to write down learning targets for each part of the standard. Readers will be given multiple examples of daily learning targets that are broken down in order to scaffold the standard into a lesson by lesson approach.

Chapter 11 – Assessing Your Learning Targets

If using learning targets fosters the most effective teaching and the most meaningful student learning (Moss and Brookhart, 2012), then readers will need a way of ensuring that the learning targets they are using are up to the task. This chapter will provide readers with six characteristics of effective learning targets that they can use to evaluate their own work review and feel assured that their final product will do what it is intended to do.

Chapter 12 – Getting Started

The focus of this book deals mostly with the process of unpacking standards and writing learning targets, because understanding how to do this work is an essential step for integrating it into one's school or classroom. However, simply understanding the work isn't going to net any results or help create high quality learning opportunities for all students. The final chapter of this book will provide some tips and advice for successfully starting this work.

Noteworthy Features

This book integrates the unpacking process alongside writing one's learning targets. These two tasks are incorporated into one easily packaged and logical process. The work for completing this process is encapsulated in five easy to follow steps that will work for any standard, in any subject, and in any grade level. In order to demonstrate the ease of this process, while also providing the reader with relevant reference material, example standards from 3rd grade reading, 6th grade math, and Biology are used throughout this book.

Work Cited

Anderson, L. W. & Krathwohl, D. R. (Eds.) (2001). *A taxonomy for learning, teaching, and assessing: A revision of Bloom's Taxonomy of educational objectives: Complete edition*. New York: Longman.

Cook-Harvey, C. M., Darling-Hammond, L., Lam, L., Mercer, C., & Roc, M. (2016). *Equity and ESSA: Leveraging educational opportunity through the every student succeeds act*. Palo Alto, CA: Learning Policy Institute.

Lachat, M. A. (1999). *Standards, equity, and cultural diversity*. Providence, RI: LAB at Brown University.

Lachat, M. A. (2004). *Standards-based instruction and assessment for english language learners*. Thousand Oaks, CA: Corwin Press.

Moss, C. M., & Brookhart, S. M. (2012) *Learning targets: Helping students aim for understanding in today's*. Alexandria, VA: ASCD.

Ravitch, D. (1995). *National standards in American education: A citizen's guide.* Washington, DC: Brookings Institution Press.

Riddle, W., (1996). Title I, Education for the Disadvantaged: Perspectives on Studies of Its Achievement Effects (CRS 96-82). Washington, DC: Congressional Research Service.

Ritchhart, R. (2002). *Intellectual Character: What it is, why it matters, and how to get it.* San Francisco: Jossey-Bass.

Ritchhart, R., Palmer, P., Church, M., & Tishman, S. (2006) Thinking routines: Establishing patterns of thinking in the classroom. AERA Conference, 2006: Harvard Graduate School of Education.

Roberts, M. J. & Erdos, G. (1993). Strategy selection and metacognition. *Educational Psychology,* 13(3–4), 259–266. doi:10.1080/0144341930130304.

Schere, M. (2001). How and why standards can improve student achievement: A conversation with robert j. marzano. *Educational Leadership,* 59, 14–18.

Shukla, D. & Dungsungnoen, P. (2016). Student's perceived level and teachers' teaching strategies of higher order thinking skills; A study on higher educational institutions in Thailand. *Journal of Education and Practice,* 7(12), 211–219.

Stevens, F. I. (1996). Closing the achievement gap: Opportunity to learn, standards, and assessment. In B. Williams (Ed.), *Closing the achievement gap: A vision for changing beliefs and practices* (pp. 77–95). Alexandria, VA: Association for Supervision and Curriculum Development.

Wolf, D. P. & Reardon, S. F. (1993, March). Equity in the design of performance assessments: A handle to wind up the tongue with? Paper presented at the Ford Foundation National Symposium on Equity and Education Testing and Assessment, Washington, DC.

# All Hands-on Deck

 ## Introduction

It is widely known, but not widely practiced, that if one is involved in the work to complete a specific project or resource then they will be more inclined to fully understand the value of the resource and then actually use the resource. It should therefore come as no surprise that the first step to understanding the process of unpacking learning targets rests in understanding who should be involved and how to get them involved. We can begin to answer this by asking who needs this information to put it directly into practice, and who needs this information to support others in its use.

Direct Involvement

The value of unpacking your learning targets is most directly beneficial and applicable for classroom teachers, as they are the ones both planning and implementing classroom lessons. Because of this it is vital that teachers are directly involved in the unpacking process and that they make up the largest groups of participants.

All teachers should be involved in the unpacking process, but it is not necessary for every teacher to unpack every standard. Larry Ainsworth (2003) explains that understanding how to involve teachers in this process is also about working smarter and not harder. I fully support his recommendation that teachers need to understand the value of the unpacking process, which is gained first-hand by everyone being trained and taken through the process at least once. After this the teams can share and split up their standards among their content area; thus alleviating the individual workload. If you have a team of about six people it is completely reasonable to plan on unpacking the learning targets for a nine-week period in an hour-and-a-half to two-hour time block, for a single subject.

 ## Support Roles

Those that need to understand this process and be able to support others in its use and implementation range all the way from district-level leaders to teacher assistants, although the roles of support provided can vary from those that may assist with academic/curricular coaching to administrative support/supervision and classroom support.

Direct use	*Support*
Classroom Teachers	District-level Curriculum Personnel
	School Administration
	Instructional Facilitators/Lead Teachers
	Teacher Assistants

Not everyone in the support roles listed above "needs" to be involved in this process, but that doesn't mean that they, as well as the process, can't benefit from their involvement. Actually, when those listed in the support column are involved in this process, we can see an increase in the efficiency of implementation. In addition to aiding implementation it is also highly beneficial in providing stakeholders with an opportunity to work and learn together, building both a sense of comradery and commitment to student learning.

District Level Curriculum Personnel

It should come as no surprise that the workload from this process, just like most others, can be substantially reduced when you have multiple people and departments all working in concert toward the same goal.

Chances are that if the push for unpacking your learning targets is coming from the district level then representation from the district's curriculum department will be neck-deep in the process. However, if this is a school-based initiative then those in the district office may not even be aware that a school has engaged in this process.

As always, it's best to keep those in charge of supporting curriculum and instruction in your district in the loop when it comes to initiatives involving the curriculum and instruction. Besides, it is quite possible that the curriculum personnel at the district office may be interested or ... dare I suggest ... even excited about helping out. Remember these people live and breathe curriculum all day, every day. They love this stuff.

School Administration/Instructional Facilitator

It's recommended that either the school-level administration or the instructional facilitator/lead teacher can be an active participant with every grade level or content area during this process. However, if both a representative of the school level administration and an instructional facilitator/lead teacher can be involved, then it's even better.

Teachers may want or need guidance when going through this process, so in order to ensure that the process is done with fidelity, coaching and support should be offered. This may also give some educational leaders an opportunity to reconnect with and offer insights to standards they themselves taught while also being introduced to new ones that they may not be familiar with. This opportunity for exposure to new standards is especially important during times of new curricular adoptions. Also, considering that both school administration and instructional facilitators are responsible for leading, supporting, and coaching their teachers it is a good idea that they are familiar with the standards that the teachers are building their lessons around.

Teacher Assistants

This process is also extremely beneficial for teacher assistants who are commonly charged with assisting in lessons, and/or conducting small groups and one-on-one teacher-to-student situations. Yet despite the charge that teacher assistants must work with and educate our students they are rarely given the training and support they need to enhance their knowledge and skills, and implementation of best practices.

Just as with the involvement of district office personnel and school leadership, the involvement of teacher assistants can also be an asset to the process. Remember the goal is to help educators and teams to improve teaching and learning; as such involving all members of a team in this process will create more effective teams. Schnorr and Davern (2005) cite that effective teams operate using a shared knowledge of effective practices, shared beliefs, and a clear understanding of their role in the team.

The process of unpacking your learning targets is a part of planning lessons and instruction, and research clearly tells us that joint planning time is essential for team success and for those involved in providing instruction to the same students (Blatchford, Russell, & Webster, 2012; Schnorr & Davern, 2005).

What's the Point?

Let's be honest ... Some leaders and/or trainers may scoff, or get a little red in the face, when an employee or teacher asks "what's the point" of a particular training program. However, asking "what's the point," of this, or anything else, is a fair question that should be asked. After all, if a concrete and logical reply can't be provided as to why educators should bother to unpack their learning targets then honestly ... why should they bother? With seemingly a million other things to do why should educators spend their valuable time on this?

It just so happens (pure coincidence) that there is a myriad of logical reasons:

1. Foundation – First off, let's start with building a solid foundation. It's already obvious that you are interested in improving teaching and learning; why else would you be reading a book all about standards and learning targets? As such we can assume you already know that everything from school-wide improvement to high-quality lesson plans must have a solid foundation that drives and supports improvement and excellence.

Taking the time to incorporate the process of unpacking your learning targets serves as a catalyst for improving the depth of understanding of how all the pieces and parts are supposed to work together. This depth of understanding serves as the foundation for alignment, rigor, improved teaching/learning, and continual school improvement.

2. Alignment – Would you like to be able to guarantee the alignment of your instruction with your local, state, or national standards? Or how about the teacher down the hall? Do you feel that students should have the same learning outcomes regardless of which teacher they happen to be assigned? Do you feel that grade-level content should be the same (4th grade is 4th grade) whether a student attends school A or school B, a few miles away? Do you want to have the ability to specifically identify and target precise areas of instructional weakness? Do you want the end-of-year standardized assessments to accurately reflect the teaching and learning that occurred in your class, grade level, school, and/or district?

   If you answered yes to any of these questions, then you understand the importance of curricular and instructional alignment; the type of alignment that can easily be gained from taking the time to unpack your learning targets.

3. Rigor – It doesn't matter how rigorous one's instruction or instructional tasks are; if they are out of alignment then your instruction will never pay dividends in terms of student performance or growth data. Not only will unpacking your learning targets aid in ensuring your tasks are aligned to your standards, but it will also aid educators in thinking through each standard in a way that will establish a logical and time sensitive progression that will scaffold the acquisition of skills to better help students demonstrate mastery of their standards.

   Student Learning – The skills that students should have upon leaving any particular grade level are conveniently laid out in pretty much every industrialized nation. Now exactly what these skills are differ county-to-country, region-to-region, or state-to-state, but regardless of where they're from, all sets of standards have a few things in common; they all aim to establish educational consistency across grade levels and they are all strategically laid out to build student skills from one grade level to the next so students can start each new school year with the foundational knowledge and skills needed to more easily acquire their learning requirements. Standards also aim to help students graduate from high school prepared for success in their careers and/or college.

For example, the common core math and reading standards, which are implemented in the majority of states within the US, specifically cite that the intent of

> These learning goals outline what a student should know and be able to do at the end of each grade. The standards were created to ensure that all students graduate from high school with the skills and knowledge necessary to succeed in college, career, and life, regardless of where they live.
> (Retrieved from http://www.corestandards.org/about-the-standards/)

The national curriculum for the United Kingdom plainly states that its purpose is to ensure that "children learn the same things," and that it covers "the standards children should reach in each subject." (Retrieved from https://www.gov.uk/national-curriculum.)

4. Professional Learning Communities (PLCs) – The process of unpacking your learning targets is a foundational component of the PLC process. Understanding how to work through the foundational components necessary to sustain and promote high functioning PLCs can help teams to avoid many unnecessary problems. Unpacking your learning targets will help to ensure that your PLC(s) are accurately targeting the appropriate learning concepts in both their lessons and their common assessments (McWherter, 2017).

   PLCs put an emphasis on improving teacher instruction and student learning through the collaborative efforts from information that teachers gain from their common assessments. So, this means that if the common assessment the teachers are using is not properly aligned to the standard(s) it is meant to assess, then the team will be responding to inappropriate and inaccurate data, which would be a waste of both time and resources for both teachers and students.

5. Minimal Time Investment – This is an efficient process that teachers/teams can use to fully unpack their learning targets for a 9-week period in approximately an hour-and-a-half. The instructional focus and alignment that can result from such an insignificant investment of time is unparalleled.

Conclusion

Although most classroom teachers are wholly capable of individually taking the resources and information in this book to improve the focus, alignment, and efficiency of their lessons, which will in turn increase their student outcomes, I would encourage you to take what you learn and share it with your teammates so their students can benefit from these practices as well. If you are a building-level or district-level coach or administrator I implore you to fully utilize your role to expand the capacity of all of those who are within your sphere of influence.

Work Cited

About the standards. (2020). Retrieved from www.corestandards.org/about-the-standards/

Ainsworth, L. (2003) *Unwrapping the standards: A simple process to make standards manageable*. Englewood, CO: The Leadership and Learning Center.

Blatchford, P., Russell, A., & Webster, R. (2012). *Reassessing the impact of teaching assistants: How research challenges practice and policy*. Oxon: Routledge.

McWherter, S. (2017). *A roadmap to plc success*. New York, NY: Routledge.

The national curriculum. (2020), Retrieved from www.gov.uk/national-curriculum

Schnorr, F. & Davern, L. (2005). Creating exemplary literacy classrooms through the power of teaming. *International Reading Association*, 58(6), 494–506.

2 Standards

Introduction

Many people dream of flying, however most of us have very few options to achieve this outside of riding in a passenger airplane. However, not everyone who wishes to fly chooses to be constrained by conventional methods. One such case occurred in the summer of 1982, when a man the media dubbed as Lawnchair Larry did something that you couldn't pay most people to do. Or at least most people with any decent amount of self-preservation.

I feel that it's safe to say that, unlike most of us, self-preservation was not an issue Larry had. With the help of a few friends, Larry tied 42 weather balloons to an aluminum lawnchair. To Larry the idea probably seemed simple, and he thought that he was well-prepared to fly his lawnchair. After all he did not "take off" without bringing some essential items: a CB radio in case he got into trouble, a pellet gun to shoot his balloons in order to land, a parachute in case he needed to jump off, and jugs of water that he strapped to the chair to assist with stability. He even had the foresight to bring along some beer and sandwiches (I would consider this the best part of his plan).By all accounts Larry seemed prepared, but as many people well know, when it comes to planning the devil is in the details.

Larry later told the media that he only initially intended to float up about 30 feet before leveling off, and then drift to the Rocky Mountains, if he was lucky. However, due to either a miscalculation in the lifting capacity of his weather balloons, or perhaps a total lack of any calculation in the first place, Lawnchair Larry shot up to an altitude of approximately 16,000 feet at an ascension rate of 1000 feet per minute. At this height

Larry was concerned of shooting out the balloons due to the possibility of it unbalancing his chair, but with no other options, he began to carefully remove some of the balloons. He was reportedly able to shoot out three balloons and was likely beginning to feel a sense of relief, and maybe even hope. Perhaps he could still get out of this situation alive, at least that was before a combination of the cold and dizziness, due to the thin air at such high altitudes, caused Larry to drop his pellet gun.

Larry floated for about 14 hours, and as the sun faded and night began to set, Larry found himself drifting out to sea three miles above the ground. Luckily Larry was spotted by some commercial airlines and a helicopter was able to drop a line from above him and pull him back over land. Even luckier still, Larry was able to "land" by getting tangled in some power lines in Long Beach, CA, and was miraculously not electrocuted because the plastic tethers that were tangled did not conduct the electricity to his metal chair. After the city cut the power to the lines, Larry was able to walk away from his ill-advised experience with his life and only $1,500 in fines (Littlejohn, 2009; Mikkelson, 2005).

What Does Lawnchair Larry Have to Do With Standards?

Teachers that plan their instruction without knowing and unpacking their standards are the educational equivalent of Lawnchair Larry; although their feet may be planted firmly in the classroom, they might as well be drifting through the clouds. I have no doubt that these teachers are still well-intentioned and they likely plan for different eventualities (pellet gun, beer, sandwiches), but what they will always be missing is clear direction. It doesn't matter how good a lesson is or how talented a teacher is; if the instruction is not aligned to the appropriate standards then the students will be unprepared for the next step in their educational journey.

In keeping with the aviation theme, your standards are the waypoints of your map and they determine the direction, altitude, and distance of your lessons. Without them you will most likely just find your instruction misaligned and floating over a proverbial ocean. But with so many different waypoints (standards) to teach, how can educators find the time to navigate all of them in a single academic year?

It Sure Is Crowded in Here

In response to the vast number of standards that educators are responsible for teaching, there is a highly technical and astute saying that I would like you to take a moment to ponder ... "Have you ever wanted to beat your head against a wall?"

Usually this saying accompanies a moment or period of frustration over a problem or circumstance, particularly when there is a known solution for the stated problem/circumstance. Oftentimes at least one of the parties involved in the decision-making process is being particularly obstinate and is creating unnecessary roadblocks or refusing to bend on a particular and often crucial point. Therefore, making everyone's life far more difficult than it needs to be.

We have all known people or had experiences with the relevant "powers that be" that have driven us to either say or think something similar to "Have you ever wanted to beat your head against a wall?". Hopefully none of you have actually attempted to solve a problem that way, as I promise the end result would be highly predictable. However, it does beg the question of why there are so many standards that we must take the time to identify "power standards".

The particular problem of having too many instructional standards has been well-known for quite some time and has been equally well-documented. This is an issue that has been formally identified by countless teachers and administrators as well as leaders in our field such as Dr. Douglas Reeves (1997, 2005), Dr. Robert Marzano (2001), and Larry Ainsworth (2010, 2014).

In response to this problem the term power standard was formally coined by Dr. Reeves, over 20 years ago, in his book *Accountability in Action* (1997). So, what is a power standard and why is it/are they important? Just as the name prescribes, a power standard has a weighted significance or priority over some of the other standards due to the importance of the knowledge or skill they address, their influence on a student's continued success in their current grade level, and as a foundational skill in their future grade levels.

In 2001 Marzano shared his belief to Educational Leadership that the current standards needed to be reduced by approximately two-thirds. At the time Marzano shared this there were approximately 130 standards across 14 different subject areas, and he estimated that students would need an additional 10 years of schooling in order to acquire all the skills.

Nine years after Marzano stated this, Larry Ainsworth (2010) shared examples that outlined state standards by grade level. Ainsworth found that grades k-8 still had between 62–110 Language Arts standards.

Now let's fast forward to the present day, nearly 20 years after Marzano shared that there were too many standards and that it was not possible for teachers to teach them all. With most states utilizing the common core curriculum it would appear that we are on the right track to meeting Marzano's recommendation and at first glance there appear to be between 42 and 48 Language Arts standards in k-8. It only took 20 years, but who cares, let's celebrate!!! Or not ... on closer investigation many of these existing standards have multiple sub-standards, which actually brings the total number of standards for k-8 Language Arts to between 73 and 91.

Are We Any Better off Now Than We Were 20 Years Ago?

The simple answer to that question is yes, on average there are indeed fewer standards than there used to be and the common core, and other state standards, tend to be much better written than their predecessors. Regardless of one's perceptions on how some of the common core is taught, the bottom line is these standards are clearer, more rigorous, and have a more concise grade-to-grade vertical alignment than their predecessors (Ainsworth, 2010).

However, due to the sheer number of standards that educators must contend with, prioritization of the standards is a necessity. When a student has skill deficits in their priority standards from previous years, these deficits become compounded and then eventually exasperated when they are introduced to new material that requires foundational knowledge and/or skills to from a previous grade level or content area. Often this scaffolding occurs within the same grade level, but in these circumstances a teacher still has ample time to address the learning deficits prior to the end of the school year. The mastery of power standards has a prevailing influence in determining a student's likelihood of success from one grade level to the next, hence the name "power" standard.

Shifting Through the Clutter

With so many standards to teach it is an absolute impossibility to dedicate the same amount of time and energy to every standard. This can be easily articulated through a simple example – if you have 90 standards to teach and you work in a district with a traditional 180-day student calendar that would mean that you are teaching a new standard every other day, with no exceptions. Forget inclement weather days, assessments, classroom celebrations, assemblies, sick days … plainly stated this is a logistical impossibility.

It could easily be for this reason alone that Dr. Reeves (2005) was able to logically debate the need to identify power standards and that Larry Ainsworth (2010, 2013, 2014) has published multiple works on the importance of, and how to prioritize standards. The grim reality is that no matter how you do the math there is simply not enough time to properly teach all of the standards.

Ainsworth (2010) provides a brief overview of the steps involved in prioritizing your standards by breaking the process down into seven steps.

> **Step one:** Identify approximately one third of a course or subject standards (based on Marzano's (2001) recommendation) using a previously agreed upon selection criteria based upon endurance, leverage, foundation for future learning, and emphasis on standardized tests.
>
> **Step two**: Reference and align item analysis for any end-of-year or high stakes tests to identified standards.
>
> **Step three:** Chart and appropriately label all of the identified standards along with the full text of the standard (ex. RL 3.1 Ask and answer questions to demonstrate understanding of a text, referring explicitly to the text as the basis for the answers.).
>
> **Step four:** Sequence and then vertically align the standard of each grade level or course. Examine overlaps and gaps, making necessary adjustments of the selected standards to insure appropriate alignment both within each grade level and to the grade level above and below it.

Step five: Collect feedback on this first draft from your educational professionals (teachers, admin, curriculum facilitators, lead teachers, etc.).

Step six: Create a second draft based on the feedback and compile a document that contains all the identified power/priority standards along with their supporting standards.

Step seven: Identify interdisciplinary standards that can be incorporated and supported in all grade levels/content areas.

Conclusion

The purpose of this chapter is not to make you an expert on recognizing power standards, or even give you the tools to help you fake it. It is simply to grant you an awareness and understanding that you can't do it all and that you can't teach everything in isolation. There are many standards that have to be taught alongside others and you have to use your time wisely in order to ensure you have given your students the tools they need for continued success. Learning to identify your power standards should be a priority for any educator, school, or district trying to be more efficient through both horizontal (grade level) and vertical alignment.

Work Cited

Ainsworth, L. (2010) *Rigorous curriculum design: How to create curricular units that align standards, instruction, and assessment.* Englewood, CO: The Leadership and Learning Center.

Ainsworth, L. (2013) *Prioritizing the common core: Identifying specific standards to emphasize the most.* Boston MA: Houghton Mifflin Harcourt.

Ainsworth, L. (2014) *Power standards: Identifying the standards that matter most.* Boston, MA: Houghton Mifflin Harcourt.

Littlejohn, D. (2009) Remember when sp man ballooned in 1982? Retrieved from www.presstelegram.com/2009/10/15/remember-when-sp-man-ballooned-in-1982/. 2/24/2020

Marzano, R. & Pollock, J. (2001) *Classroom instruction that works: Research-Based strategies for increasing student achievement.* Alexandria, VA: Association for Supervision and Curriculum Development.

Mikkelson, D. (2005) Up, up, and away: Did larry walters soar above los angeles in a lawn chair attached to helium weather balloons? Retrieved from www.snopes.com/fact-check/up-up-and-away/. 2/24/2020

Reeves, D. (1997) *Accountability in Action: A blue print for learning organizations.* Boston MA: Houghton Mifflin Harcourt.

Reeves, D. (2005) *Accountability in Action: A blue print for learning organizations.* 2nd edition. Boston MA: Houghton Mifflin Harcourt.

Schere, M. (2001). How and why standards can improve student achievement: A conversation with robert j. marzano. *Educational Leadership,* 59, 14–18.

What Is a Learning Target?

Introduction

Oftentimes when we observe learning targets in a classroom they may not be listed under the heading "Learning Target"; rather they will be displayed under the heading "Essential Question", "I can statement", or occasionally "Big Idea". However all of these, save for the big idea, each constitute learning targets in their own right, only differing in their stylized approach to identifying what the students need to learn from the lesson.

Now I know that some individuals who utilize Essential Questions may want to burn me at the stake for voicing such heresy, but before you start making a woodpile it is important to be aware that neither the process nor the rationale for unpacking your learning targets are any different for either traditional "I can" statements or Essential Questions.

Jay McTighe and Grant Wiggins, both leaders in the arena of Essential Questions, specifically state that the content goals (Standards) should be unpacked as part of the process of writing corresponding Essential Questions for each of the standards. This is because some of the key rationalizations for writing Essential Questions include the clarification of standards for teachers and a clear focal point/lesson orientation for students (McTighe, J; Wiggins, G; 2013). This means that the logical timing for writing either traditional Learning Targets or Essential Questions occurs while the corresponding standard(s) are being unpacked.

A Learning Target Is Not ...

Before we talk about what a learning target is let us discuss what it is not. A simplified theory of this is expressed by Moss and Brookhart (2012), who state that "a learning target is not an instructional objective." Instructional objectives are written from the teacher's point of view with the purpose of unifying student outcomes across a series of related lessons or an entire unit. Instructional objectives highlight what learning goals the lesson-specific learning targets are scaffolded to bring the students to.

You now know that a learning target is not the same as an instructional objective, but learning targets and instructional objectives are both derived from your standards. You also know that they are used to break apart standards, or instructional objectives, into easily scaffolded fragments that are used to bring students to mastery of a standard(s) in a sequenced lesson-by-lesson approach.

A learning target is not abstract. Learning targets are meant to be clear and concise, and capture the learning that is supposed to be taking place in a given lesson, increasing academic transparency for all stakeholders.

A learning target is not a secret ... remove any aspirations you may have to be an international spy. Learning targets are meant to be shared with your students, peers, and even parents.

A Learning Target Is ...

After leaving the office the other day I picked my son up from his afterschool care. I received the customary hug and the usual story about what he had just been doing and who he had been playing with. Once we got into the car we settled into the all too familiar conversation where I try, almost always in vain, to have him tell me about what he learned that day. He avoids my question(s) like the plague and instead asks me if I want to hear about what he had for lunch and then what his special was (i.e. gym, art, music etc.). He then proceeds to tell me exactly what he thought of his school lunch and how he ate all of his vegetables, then he tells me all about a new math game that he played in his computer class, and how many points he earned. Then before I can restate a variant of my original question he quickly tries to pivot the conversation by asking me how my day was, or what we are going to have for dinner ... "well now hang on just a minute," I say, "what did you guys do in class? Did you learn anything new? Did you do anything fun?" "Ummmm ... " he says, as he looks out the window impatiently waiting for this conversation to end. "Well?" I say ... more silence ... then he finally replies, "No, I don't think we learned anything new today."

So after more than 100 days into the school year, according to his recollection, he has not learned anything new ... ever. Yeah, right. Now obviously we can assume this to be a classic rendition of the all too common – what did you learn today/nothing – conversation that parents have been having with their children ever since the first schoolhouse was created.

So why bother with the story of my son's apparent belief that he hasn't learned anything all year? And what do learning targets have to do with this? The answer is everything.

Picture learning targets not only as the final destination for a lesson or lesson set, but also as the proverbial tour guide. At the beginning of the lesson the teacher reviews the learning target with the class, then they continue to reference the learning target throughout the lesson, and finally end the lesson by reviewing the learning target and completing a brief knowledge or skill check to ensure that the students attained the desired knowledge or skills that the lesson was intended to impart.

Imagine the clarity this could bring students when they are trying to think of or articulate what they learned. What a difference reviewing a learning target before, during, and after a lesson would make ... now imagine if teachers would share these with parents to assist in facilitating a better home-to-school connection.

When teachers use learning targets they need to ensure that they are in student-friendly language ... no, this doesn't mean that you must dumb it down, rather it should be grade level appropriate, and should also include appropriate content vocabulary. The purpose for framing learning targets in student-friendly language is so that – you guessed it! – students can understand them. This novel idea is firmly planted in in the research-based practice of common sense, and hopefully needs no detailed explanation. Remember, learning targets are to be routinely shared with the students, as such students need to be able to understand them.

What Is a Learning Target?

Many teachers may forget that the learning target needs to be continually referenced throughout the lesson, and that each lesson should be clearly scaffolded to bring the students to the learning objective(s) in the target. Beginning each lesson by introducing the learning target, referencing it at least once during the lesson, and ending the lesson with some type of check for understating or exit ticket is a good way to keep your lessons targeted and to ensure that students have a clear understanding of their learning goal for that day. These steps are easy to forget if a lesson is not built around the learning target.

There are two specific types of learning targets: *overarching* and *lesson-specific*. Lesson-specific learning targets are crafted for a single lesson in order to provide the scaffolded chunks that will give students the knowledge and skills they need to master the *overarching* learning target. They are the separate pieces that are put together to make the whole picture. These will be discussed in greater detail in Chapter 10.

> Let's review ... A Learning Target is:
> a lesson-sized chunk of information;
> written in student friendly language;
> shared with students at the beginning, throughout, and then reviewed at the end of a lesson;
> centered around the standard(s) that the teacher is basing his/her lesson on.

A lesson-specific learning target builds upon the learning target from the previous lesson, and learning targets are strategically crafted to continually build upon each other in order to help students achieve an overarching skill, or skills that are encapsulated by standards.

Why Should You Write Learning Targets?

So now that we've covered what a learning target is and is not, let's review a basic question you may have, or one you are likely to be asked: "Why should I write learning targets?" In their book, *The 12 Touchstones of Good Teaching*, Bryan Goodwin and Elizabeth Ross Hubbell state that teachers need to narrow standards into a series of concrete steps that students can accomplish during a lesson or lesson set. They go on to explain what commonly happens when they ask students what they are learning as part of their school walkthrough protocols.

> Very often, unless the teacher has been purposeful in communicating the learning objective, students almost invariably answer with the activity they are doing rather than the learning objective that activity supports. This is sometimes reinforced by the fact that an agenda has been posted that includes the activity, but not necessarily the learning objectives tied to that activity.
>
> (pg. 26)

This sounds very reminiscent of why my son always tells me that he didn't learn anything at school.

Learning Targets Guide Students

Learning targets will help your students to become active participants in their own learning, and will assist them in connecting the classroom activities to the learning objective/target. Properly utilizing learning targets makes the learning expectations clear for your students and enables the necessary support structures to be implemented.

Learning Targets Guide Teachers

When teachers properly use learning targets that are aligned to their standard(s), they are able to maintain appropriate pacing while also avoiding spending an obsessive amount of time on a particular unit or concept that they just happen to be extremely passionate about. They are also able to ensure that appropriate time is spent on the content that they may have only glossed over in the past, either due to personal disinterest or simply due to a disconnect from the actual depth of the subject matter.

Learning targets help teachers to begin each lesson with the end in mind, while avoiding aimless coverage and aimless activities (Goodwin & Ross Hubbell, 2013). They guide educators to home in on exactly what it is they want students to learn, and then plan for exactly how they are going to teach it, what activities they will use, and how students will demonstrate that they have mastered it.

Learning Targets Help to Set Goals

Most children – and many adults – have trouble with goal setting. This is largely because the goals that people try to make for themselves are simply too big, are set too far in the future, or are way too general and therefore have little accountability. Now there is nothing wrong with setting ambitious or grand goals for yourself. But if the duration of time needed to achieve one's goal is too far out or if the goal is too vague, then the likelihood of success can be greatly diminished. Having frequent short-term goals that will eventually lead you to your desired outcome will greatly increase your likelihood of success.

Using learning targets is no different than having a series of short-term goals for both you and your students that will eventually lead both you and them to the desired outcome.

How many people do you know who make New Year's Resolutions to lose weight or to exercise more? Perhaps you are one of these people? If so, you may be part of the 80% who, according to mental health clinician Dr. Shainna Alli (2018), fail or give up on their goal by February. So why are so many people unsuccessful when it comes to meeting or maintaining their New Year's Resolutions?

Jonathan Alpert, a psychotherapist and author of *Be Fearless: Change Your Life in 28 Days*, stated the three biggest reasons why people fail to meet their New Year's Resolutions.

1. Your goal isn't specific enough.

Alpert states that it's easier to quit or give up on a goal when your desired outcome is vague. He suggests having a timeline and to think of short-term, medium-term, and long-term benchmarks to keep yourself on track.

Instead of saying "I'm going to exercise more this year" or "I'm going to start going to the gym," try saying "I'm going to go to the gym three times a week for 45 minutes each time for the month of January". Instead of saying "I'm going to start eating more healthily" try saying "I'm going to drink only water and coffee/tea for the next 30 days". Then after you achieve these short-term goals, make a new goal to continue pushing yourself to exercise or eat healthy.

2. Your goal isn't framed in a positive nature.

Goals should be framed in a positive nature and refrain from focusing on the behavior you are trying to avoid; for example, if you want to cut soda out of your diet, don't make a goal *saying* you're going to cut soda out of your diet, because it will constantly remind you of what you're trying to avoid. Instead, make a goal to drink more water or other healthy alternatives.

Learning targets generally start out with the phrase "I can ... " This is a good start to being positive; just be sure not to conclude your "I can" statement with the behavior you are trying to avoid, for instance "I can stop making farting noises in Ms. Branch's classroom," as this would only encourage you to continue those behaviors, guided by youthful immaturity.

3. Your goal isn't about you.

Alpert states that a major obstacle that hinders our success is that that we tend to make goals based on what we think others may expect of us.

You don't make learning targets based on what you think or believe a peer mentor may want you to teach, and you shouldn't be planning lessons on topics just to impress your administrator. Rather, lessons are designed to address specific learning targets that are planted firmly in the standard(s) that they are designed to teach. Everything we do as educators is based on what is most appropriate for our students, but the focal point of a learning target or instructional standard starts with the teacher. It is then the teacher's purpose to instruct and facilitate learning in the classroom, because the students won't learn it without you.

So do learning targets make the mark for increasing the likelihood of meeting your classroom instructional goals? Let's see ...

1. **Specific short-term goals** – Learning targets are highly focused, lesson-specific, and unit-specific.
2. **Positive** – "I can … " Need I say more?
3. **About you** – Learning targets are made from the standards that *you* are responsible for teaching

Conclusion

For those of you who want a surefire way to build a springboard for continued student learning – start with the foundation. Before you start talking about rigor, student discourse, cooperative learning, technology integration or any other trendy educational topic (although all are important in their own right, and do need to be discussed and integrated to continue increasing student achievement), you should know that most struggling or failing schools are in the position they are because students are not receiving consistent high quality instruction aligned to the standards they are being assessed on. Karen Chenoweth (2007) plainly states that schools must clearly define what students should be learning at every grade level and ensure that it gets taught every day.

Research has indicated that the school-level variable that most strongly correlates to student achievement can be determined by the extent to which a school clearly articulates the curriculum, monitors that the curriculum is taught, and then ensures that its curriculum is aligned to any high stakes assessments (Goodwin & Ross Hubbell, 2013; Marzano, 2000). As Goodwin and Ross Hubble (2013) point out:

> The not so surprising implication of this research is that students do better on tests when they've been taught what's being tested. Hence, one of the keyways that low-performing schools nationwide have dramatically improved their performance is by getting their curriculum in order.

Before you start focusing on the mid- or upper-levels of instructional refinement, ensure that the foundation you are working from is firmly aligned to the learning objectives set by the content standards. Otherwise, although you may see improvements in instructional delivery and perceived student learning, these gains may not transfer to improvement on your accountability measures.

Although there are a variety of reasons and even more excuses for neglecting instructional alignment, the simple fact remains that students are going to learn what you teach them. This is what you have to ask yourself; is what I am teaching the same as what my students are being tested on?

Work Cited

Alli, S. (2018) Why New Year's Resolutions fail: Four common ways you may be standing in the way of your personal growth. Retrieved from www.psychologytoday.com/us/blog/modern-mentality/201812/why-new-years-resolutions-fail

Alpert, J. & Bowman, A. (2019). *Be fearless: Change your life in 28 days*. New York, NY: Hachette Book Group.

Chenoweth, K. (2007). *It's being done: Academic success in unexpected schools*. Cambridge, MA: Harvard Education Press.

Goodwin, B. & Ross Hubbell, E. (2013). *The 12 touchstones of good teaching: A checklist for staying focused everyday*. Alexandria, VA: ASCD.

Marzano, R. J. (2000). *A new era of school reform: Going where the research takes us*. Aurora, CO: Mid-continent Research for Education and Learning.

McTighe, J. & Wiggins, G. (2013). *Essential questions: Opening the doors to student understanding*. Alexandria, VA: ASCD.

Moss, C. M. & Brookhart, S. M. (2012). *Learning targets: Helping students aim for understanding in today's*. Alexandria, VA: ASCD.

4 | Process

Introduction

I'm not going to say that there is only one method for unpacking your learning targets, or that the process described in this resource is the only way, or even the best way. However, I will say that I believe this to be one of the simplest and most user-friendly methods. Over the years I have worked with a variety of educators to refine this process and have utilized this framework with great success.

The steps are broken down into five sections. A brief overview for each section is provided below. Each question/task in this framework is designed to systematically assist the educator(s) through the unpacking process in a streamlined approach. Chapters 4–8 offer a thorough explanation and examples, and will walk you through each of the steps in this process.

Follow the Steps

Standard Deconstruction

The process for unpacking a chosen standard must start with the central component of breaking down a standard to its essential words and phrases while also paying particular attention to the conjunctions and punctuation within the standard. Doing this allows educators to get to the central focus of the standard.

Word Wise

Even after a standard has been broken down to its essential words and phrases, it is incorrect to assume that everyone defines and understands the words and terms the same way. Not only is it extremely important to make sure that the team is operating with the same understandings, but we must also ensure that the team's assumed definition(s) and understandings align with that of the authors of the standard. Otherwise the instruction that follows may be perfectly aligned in a school but completely misaligned to state, local, or national intent.

Cut the Fluff

This section of the template helps educators to focus on the basic premise of the chosen standard by reconstructing the essential words and phrases. The focus here remains specifically on what the students need to be able to do in a simple and easy to understand manner.

Standard Reconstruction

When an individual has the ability to explain a standard in their own words, it usually indicates that they have comprehensive understanding of it. After completing steps 1–4, individuals/teams should have the breadth/scope of understanding to reword the standard while still capturing its purpose and intent. In addition to demonstrating a comprehensive understanding, reconstructing the standard will also allow others to more easily assimilate the standard in the future. This is especially important since it is not likely that every member of the grade level will have the time to individually unpack every standard.

Process

Standard #_____

Standard - Record chosen standard
_____
_____
_____

Standard Deconstructon - Read your chosen standard and reduce it to just its essential words/ phrases.
_____
_____
_____

Punctuation Pitfalls: Reread your standard - Consider all the punctuation signs and/or conjunctions- Think about how it effects your understanding of the standard - Share your thinking

Word Wise - Examine the key words and phrases in the standard. What word(s) do you want to pullout for discussion and/or clarification – Look up and define chosen word(s).

_____ - _____

_____ - _____

Cut the Fluff: Reread your grade level standard. Condense and summarize the standard (what do the students need to be able to do, and how)

    What - _____

    How - _____

Standard Reconstruction: Focusing on what your students are supposed to do and how they are supposed to do it write an explanation and/ or paraphrase the standard in your own words.
_____
_____
_____

Learning Targets - Create learning targets for the standard

    Overarching learning target (reference "Standard Reconstruction")
_____

    Lesson specific Learning targets (reference "Cut the Fluff")

Day 1 - _____
Day 2 - _____
Day 3 - _____
Day 4 - _____

Figure 4.1 Unpacking Template

Learning Targets

*Do not skip this step or leave it for "later". There is no better time to write your corresponding learning targets then when you are most familiar with a standard. This step has two parts; the first is to create the overarching learning target. This frames the intent of the standard into something the students should be able to do, answer, demonstrate, or explain at the end of a series of lessons. The second step is to write down learning targets for each part of the standard. In essence, you are breaking down and scaffolding the standard into a lesson-by-lesson approach. This is done by putting into words what the students need to be able to do each day, in order to build them up to the point where they have the foundational knowledge/skills to demonstrate mastery of the standard.

Conclusion

I believe that making efforts to simplify any process in order to best achieve its core function is a powerful asset when perusing school growth and instructional improvement to both educational leaders and classroom teachers. Working smarter and not harder assists all parties in increasing efficiency and productivity, while also helping to increase the likelihood that the educators one is trying to help will buy into or even attempt something new. This framework and its process is intentionally meant to be so simple that any team or individual can implement it, while being so logical that any team or individual will be able to see the value in it. The figure below (Figure 4.1) shows a template depicting all of the steps as they might appear on an unpacking document.

Standard Deconstruction

 ## Introduction

A critical first step to gaining a more accurate insight of a standard is to reduce the standard to its essential or key words. This step is fairly simple and straightforward and will give you a solid frame of reference that will keep you focused and on track when moving through the other steps in this process. In this chapter you will also be introduced to three standards that will be used as exemplars throughout the rest of this book in order to help guide you through this process. However, please keep in mind that this process will work for any standard in any subject, and in any grade level. The example standards used in this book are merely to provide you with a visual reference of this process.

 ## Identifying Key Words

There are a few different ways to go about identifying key words/phrases in a standard, but most importantly the identification process revolves around words that are descriptive and provide direction to the educator. As a guiding principal, Ainsworth (2003) recommends that educators pay special attention to the nouns and verbs in the standard they are working with. The nouns/noun phrases represent the concepts within the standard that students will need to understand or master in order to complete the skill(s)/(verb(s)) that they will need to demonstrate.

Simply stated, within a standard
Nouns = Concepts
Verbs = Skills

To give you a quick frame of reference, the chart below provides a few examples of some regularly occurring concepts and skills that can be found in many standards.

In addition to being able to identify the concepts and skills within a standard, it is also pivotal to pay close attention to the conjunctions within a standard and the use of the words such as "and"/"or", as they can have rather large implications.

Nouns/Concepts	Verbs/Skills
Number sense, text complexity, scaffolding, whole number, multiplication, long and short vowels, main idea, sequence, numerator	Recognize, demonstrate, apply, ask, compare, explain, identify, answer, understand, comprehend, distinguish

By focusing on these essential words and phrases, educators will be able to more accurately assess each of the standards without getting tied up in overly wordy or confusing standards. This is an important first step because identifying the concepts, skills, and conjunctions within a standard makes the task of reducing your selected standard to its essential words quite simple. Identifying these essential words and phrases also provides a stable and coherent skeleton of the standard that is easily referenced throughout the unpacking process.

Sample Standards

Let's take a look at the three sample standards that will be used as examples throughout the following steps.

Example 1 – 3rd Grade Reading

RI3.1 – Ask and answer questions to demonstrate understanding of a text, referring explicitly to the text as the basis for the answers.

Standard Deconstruction

Example 2 – 7th Grade Math

7G.A.2 – Draw (freehand, with a ruler and protractor, and with technology) geometric shapes with given conditions. Focus on constructing triangles from three measures of angles or sides, noticing when the conditions determine a unique triangle, more than one triangle, or no triangle.

Example 3 – Biology

Bio.2.2.1 – Infer how human activities (including population growth, pollution, global warming, burning of fossil fuels, habitat destruction and introduction of non-native species) may impact the environment.

Similar to the standards you are sure to encounter, in your own grade level or content area, the exemplar standards are meant to represent an array of depth and complexity. Some of the standards you work with will be pretty straightforward, others will be instantly recognizable as more complex, and some of them may at first appear simple, but have more depth than you first assumed.

Getting Started

You are welcome to read through each of the steps and then practice using these same standard(s). I would also encourage you to take the time to work through one of your own standards simultaneously as you read through the steps in each chapter. If you work through using any of the example standards provided in the previous section, simply cover up the Figures that show the completed work until you have given it a try, then you can compare your responses to those in this book. If you decide to use one of your own standards, simply cite the example standards as reference guides.

Under each of the steps there will be a section titled Work Along; the directions in each of these sections will help guide you through the process whether you are working simultaneously as you are reading or whether you decide to work through the process after you have read the book. All of the Work Along sections can also be found in the Appendix for easy reference.

Standard Deconstruction

To assist you in working through this process, the template is available for you to print out at www.routledge.com/products/ and is listed as Figure 3.1. Remember that the best way to learn this process is to practice going through it, just as the best way to learn any work is to do the work. Plunging into work that you aren't necessarily experienced or good at are excellent traits of a growth mindset (Dewick, 2006). If you happen to be off the mark, who cares? You will become more fluent and the process will become easier the more you do it.

If you wish to try your hand at unpacking one of your own standards as you're reading, just cover up the figures for each section that show the completed step, read the instructions for each section, and give it a shot.

Step One

First identify the standard you or your group is going to unpack. You should be selecting a standard that is already identified by either your district curriculum office or by your state/region as being a priority.

If you are choosing to work along with me, I am going to start with the example standard for Third Grade Reading provided in the previous section.

"Ask and answer questions to demonstrate understanding of a text, referring explicitly to the text as the basis for the answers."

> **Work Along**
>
> Either rewrite your standard on your template, if you choose to, or just reference it from its original source.

Step Two

The next step is to identify the essential words and phrases from the standard and write them down in the space provided under "Standard Deconstruction" on the template.

Standard Deconstruction

Do this by identifying key words/phrases in a standard that are descriptive and provide specific direction to the educator as to what the student has to do and how they will do it.

At times you will find that most or all of the words/phrases in a standard are essential. As such it helps to break these words and phrases into chunks, similar to the example in Figure 4.2.

> **Work Along**
>
> Go ahead and re-read the standard a few times and identify the concepts that you think students will need to understand, and how they will demonstrate their understanding.
>
> *If you are unsure of how to get started, reference Figure 4.1 to help you identity some essential words.

Step Three

The next step is to identify any specific punctuation and/or conjunctions that may influence one's understanding of a standard. Not all standards will have punctuation/conjunctions that need to be discussed, but when they do it is important to take a few extra seconds to take note of them.

> **Work Along**
>
> Do you see any conjunctions? if so, determine which, if any, of them influence what skill(s) a student needs to understand or how they need to demonstrate understanding.

Next, identify any punctuation within the standard (aside from the period at the end). Is the punctuation mark influencing what skill(s) a student needs to understand or how they need to demonstrate understanding?

Record your findings in the space provided under "Punctuation Pitfalls".

Standard Deconstruction

Examples

In Figures 5.1–5.3 on the following pages you can see how the essential words and phrases are circled and written below. Please note that you do not have to write out each of the standards and circle the essential words/phrases, then write them all out. That would be redundant and would fall under the category of working harder and not smarter. You can simply write the essential words and phrases from the standard in the space provided. I have provided the examples in this manner simply to illustrate the process.

Directly under each of the following examples is a walk-through description of the standard deconstruction process.

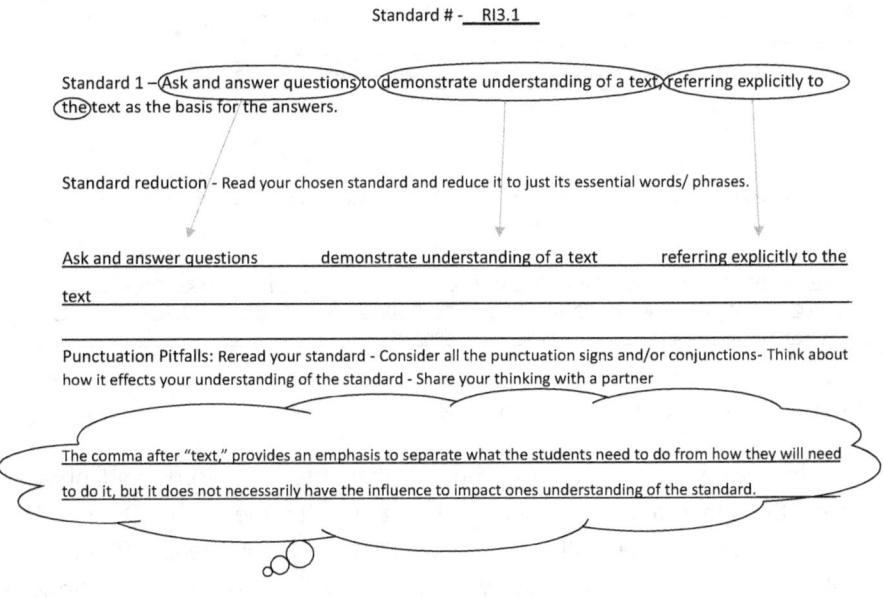

Figure 5.1 RI3.1 Standard Deconstruction

In the figure above, the essential words and phrases from standard RI.3.1 begin logically with "Ask and answer questions". This informs the teacher in what way the student(s) should be able to demonstrate proficiency of the standard. This is furthered by the phrase "demonstrate understanding of the text" which lets the teacher know what the basis is for the "questions" students should be asking and answering.

33

Standard Deconstruction

The phrase "referring explicitly to the text" informs the teacher of the concept that the students need to become proficient at referencing.

For this standard the comment under Punctuation Pitfalls is not a required piece of the unpacking process, as there is no punctuation or conjunctions that could influence one's understanding of the standard. You are sure to encounter many standards that do in fact have influential punctuation and conjunctions (as shown in the examples in the following figures) and there is no need to spend time writing out the intent of a comma that everyone can clearly and easily understand. The example here is written out for the sole purpose of showing the thought process.

Unpacking Your learning Targets
Standard # - 7G.A.2

Standard 2 - Draw freehand, with a ruler and protractor, and with technology geometric shapes with given conditions. Focus on constructing triangles from three measures of angles or sides, noticing when the conditions determine a unique triangle, more than one triangle, or no triangle.

Standard reduction - Read your chosen standard and reduce it to just its essential words/ phrases.

Draw free hand, with a ruler and protractor, and with technology geometric shapes with given conditions constructing triangles from three measures of angles or sides determine a unique triangle, more than one triangle, or no triangle

Figure 5.2 7G.A.2 Standard Deconstruction

In Figure 5.2 above, you can see that essential words and phrases from the 7th grade math standard begins with the verb "Draw." The action *to draw* specifically dictates what must be completed. This is then followed with additional clarity provided by the description of *how* to draw: "freehand, with a ruler and protractor, and with technology," and then the general guidelines for what to draw: "geometric shapes with given conditions". This informs us that students are not just drawing random squares and triangles, but rather they are given specific "conditions" or parameters such as measures of angles and/or sides to use when drawing their geometric shapes.

The next phrase further informs the educator that even though students should practice drawing a variety of geometric shapes, there should be an overt focus on "constructing triangles from three measures of angles or sides".

Lastly the standard tells us that students should be able to determine when the shape they have drawn is a "unique triangle," could be "more than one triangle," or is "no triangle."

Unpacking Your learning Targets
Standard # - Bio.2.2.1

Standard 3 - Infer how human activities (including population growth, pollution, global warming, burning of fossil fuels, habitat destruction and introduction of nonnative species) may impact the environment.

Standard reduction - Read your chosen standard and reduce it to just its essential words/ phrases.

Infer how human activities may impact the environment

including population growth, pollution, global warming, burning of fossil fuels, habitat destruction and

introduction of nonnative species

Figure 5.3 Bio.2.2.1 Standard Deconstruction

From a quick glance at Figure 5.3 above, you likely already deduced that the entire Biology standard has been identified as either a key word or phrase. This will occasionally happen when you come across condensed standards where every word imparts a non-repetitive significance. For example: the verb "Infer" is only used one time in this standard. Had it been used twice we would have omitted identifying it twice, as it would have served no additional value.

In this standard the teacher is supposed to apply the directive of "infer" to "how human activities … may impact the environment". Even though the single statement "how human activities … may impact the environment" is broken apart in the standard, it would have been identified as a single key phrase had it not been divided by supporting directives.

Lastly the supporting directives inform the educator that students must be able to make their inferences based off of the specific human activities of "… population growth, pollution, global warming, burning fossil fuels, habitat destruction and introduction of non-native species".

Conclusion

If you were working along as you were reading, hopefully you felt that this step was not overly challenging and was straightforward, and guess what? That's the point! Reducing a standard to its essential words and phrases is the first step in the process of unpacking your learning targets.

Even after a standard has been broken down to its essential words and phrases, it is incorrect to assume that everyone defines and understands the words and terms the same way. Not only is it extremely important to make sure that the team is operating on the same page, but we must also ensure that their definition aligns with that of the authors of the standard. This chapter will explain why this often overlooked step is so important.

Work Cited

Ainsworth, L. (2003). *Unwrapping the standards: A simple process to make standards manageable*. Englewood, CO: The Leadership and Learning Center.

Dewick, C. (2006). *Mindset: The psychology of success*. New York: Random House.

Word Wise

 Introduction

After the essential words and phrases have been pulled out of the standard the next step in this process is to become Word Wise. This is usually one of the quickest steps in the unpacking process, but don't let this fool you into thinking that it is not equally as important as the other steps. To some it may seem silly or even a waste of time to discuss the meaning of words that we use on a regular basis in our professions, but there is not enough I can say to accentuate the importance of this step. Not only is it vital to make sure that the team is operating with the same understandings, but we must also ensure that the assumed understandings and definition of the team aligns with that of the standard (which operates on dictionary definitions). If there is a misunderstanding or misinterpretation of a word or words within a standard, the delivery of instruction that follows may be perfectly aligned in a particular grade level at a particular school while being completely misaligned to the state, local, or national intent – and therefore be consequently misaligned to any local, state, or national assessments tied to it.

 What's in a Word?

English is a complicated language with most of its vocabulary originating from Germanic, French, and Latin roots. It is full of spelling conundrums and unique grammatical examples. Spelling of words such as dough,

Word Wise

tough, and bough, for example, which are all spelled similarly but pronounced completely different. Phrasal verbs can be completely changed in meaning based on the words placed before or after them, such as the word run. We can go for a run, run over someone, run up a bill, run into a friend, run an idea by you. There is also the phenomenon of idioms, which is where a statement means something different than the meaning of the actual words used. For example, "a dime a dozen," "beat around the bush," "break a leg," "turn in for the night" (Evans, 2017).

Even for native speakers who are well-educated there are plenty of opportunities to get things turned around. Some of the most common mistakes revolve around the use of synonyms, homonyms, homophones, homographs, and heteronyms. These are words that may be different but mean the same thing, have different sounds and meanings but be spelled the same, have the same spelling and pronunciation but different meanings, or have the same pronunciation but different spellings and meanings. Figure 6.1 provides some examples of these and how they relate to each other.

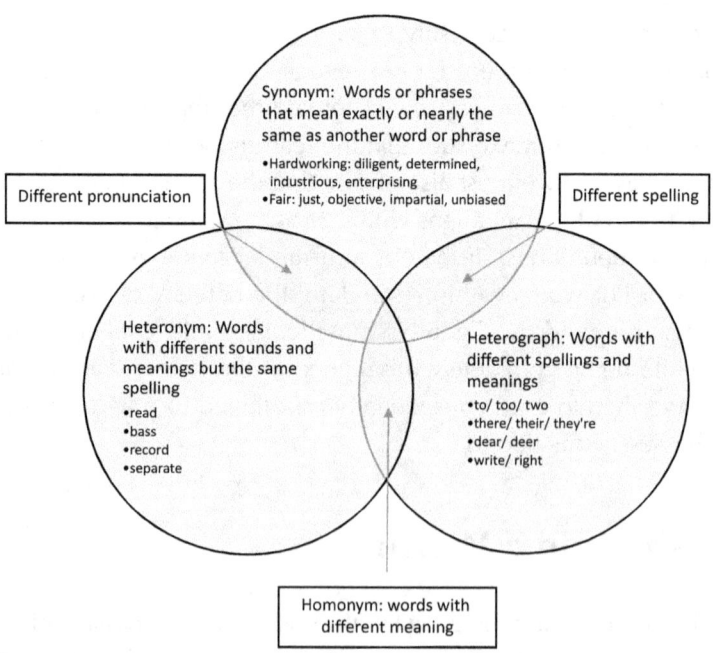

Figure 6.1 Understanding Homophones and Homographs

38

In addition to all of this there are also words and phrases people may use with the belief that everyone has the same understanding or has the same mental image in their head. Here is one familiar example I'm sure we can all relate to. Take the statement "the meeting starts at 9:00". To some people this means that they need to be there before 9:00 so the meeting can start at 9:00. To others it means be there by 9:00, and the meeting will start soon after, yet others assume it means that they need to be pulling into the parking lot around 9:00 and the meeting will probably start around 9:15.

In another short illustration to demonstrate how we can so differently interpret common words, I would like you to picture the word *cake*. Now I want you to imagine a piece of cake That's right, a piece of cake, but not just any cake – this is *your* cake, your favorite cake. Now I want you to picture every detail of your cake just as a piece is being cut and placed on a plate just for you, with fork in hand. Now I want you to imagine the texture of your cake as your fork slides through it … now smell the aromas as you bring up the first mouth-watering bite, and imagine the taste as you close your lips around it.

So what did you imagine? My cake, just in case you are curious, is a thick and moist triple chocolate with cream cheese icing, but not too much icing.

In any size group you will quickly learn how many different versions of "cake" there are, and this is true for many things. I can recall a school board I was familiar with once spent about two hours discussing what constituted a sandal as it applied to the dress code. You can do an activity like this with many different words or phrases that may not be as innately clear as one may believe. However, this and the other example highlight the importance of identifying and discussing any words or phrases in your content standards that could either be open for interpretation, or that an inexperienced teacher may not yet be as familiar with or have the same common understanding of as their veteran peers.

Word Wise

 ## Step One

The first step in this part of the process is to re-read the essential words and phrases from the Standard Reduction. You may want to read through it a couple of times in order to let the significance of each word influence your understanding of the text. Dig deep into the words and search for those words that extort a specific implication or importance. Are there words that could be subjective or have multiple meanings?

Here are the essential words and phrases from the 3rd grade reading standard used in the previous chapter.

Standard Reduction – "Ask and answer questions ... demonstrate understanding of a text ... referring explicitly to the text"

> **Work Along**
> Carefully reread the essential words and phrases from the Standard Reduction and identify the significance of each word

 ## Step 2

Now that you have taken some time to carefully reread and mentally digest each of the essential words and phrases from your standard, go ahead and write down the significant word(s) you identified in the space provided. Remember the word(s) that you selected should always impart a weighted significance to the standard, and do at least one of the following:

- Specifically dictate or influence an action
- Be content-specific vocabulary (i.e. photosynthesis, prime number, hyperbole)
- Have the potential to be easily misinterpreted or overlooked

Word Wise

> **Work Along**
>
> Write down the word(s) you identified and then look up the and record the definition(s) in the space provided

Depending on the length or complexity of a definition you may choose to paraphrase it.

 ## Examples

In Figures 6.2–6.4 on the following pages you can see that the significant words, which I pulled out of the essential words and phrases from each standard, are circled. You do not have to circle them if you don't want to; I have provided the examples in this manner in order to illustrate the process.

Unpacking Your learning Targets
Standard # - ___RI3.1___

Standard 1 – Ask and answer questions to demonstrate understanding of a text, referring explicitly to the text as the basis for the answers.

Standard Deconstruction - Read anchor Standard - Read your grade level standard - Reduce your standard to essential words and phrases

Ask and answer questions demonstrate understanding of a text referring (explicitly) to the

text
_____

Punctuation Pitfalls: Reread your standard - Consider all the punctuation signs and/or conjunctions - Think about how it effects your understanding of the standard - Share your thinking with a partner

The comma after "text," provides an emphasis to separate what the students need to do from how they will need

to do it, but it does not necessarily have the influence to impact ones understanding of the standard

Word Wise - Examine the key words and phrases in the standard. What word(s) do you want to pullout for discussion and/or clarification – Look up and define chosen word(s).

Explicitly – Fully and clearly expressed or demonstrated; leaving nothing merely implied; unequivocal

Figure 6.2 RI3.1 Word Wise

Word Wise

Directly under each of the examples is a walk-through description illustrating the meaning of each word selected.

As you can see in Figure 6.2 above, the only word I selected from the reading standard RI3.1 was "explicitly". The root word of "explicitly" is "explicit", and its use in the phrase "referring explicitly to the text" not only gives it a weighted significance to the standard, but its placement also directly influences the action that the students are supposed to demonstrate.

In addition to this, the word "explicit" can sometimes be confused with "implicit". Confusing these two words could have a disastrous impact on the alignment of a teacher's lessons, as implicit means "something that is implied, rather than expressly stated". A teacher who confuses these two words would have their class working on inferring meaning from text instead of directly pulling evidence from text, and then no matter how rigorous the classroom instruction was, the students would have altogether missed a valuable skill that would later be used as part of the scaffolded learning to assist them with inferring.

Unpacking Your learning Targets
Standard # -   7G.A.2

Standard 2 - Draw (freehand, with a ruler and protractor, and with technology) geometric shapes with given conditions. Focus on constructing triangles from three measures of angles or sides, noticing when the conditions determine a unique triangle, more than one triangle, or no triangle.

Standard Deconstruction - Read anchor Standard - Read your grade level standard - Reduce your standard to essential words

Draw free hand, with a ruler and protractor, and with technology geometric shapes

Constructing triangles from three measures of angles or sides   determine a (unique triangle) more than one triangle, or no triangle

Word Wise - Examine the key words and phrases in the standard. What word(s) do you want to pullout for discussion and/or clarification – Look up and define chosen word(s).

Unique Triangle – A triangle that can only be drawn one way. If a triangle is not unique then more than one triangle can be formed using the same measures.

Figure 6.3 7G.A.2 Word Wise

From the 7th grade Math standard, in Figure 6.3 I selected "unique triangle". In this standard unique triangle provides a weighted significance to the standard as it represents something that the students need to be able to recognize. It also represents content-specific vocabulary.

The importance of this definition would become truly realized once a teacher begins to write their lessons and plan tasks for their students to complete. This is especially true since a unique triangle can appear in any number of ways depending on the given conditions and can be any type of triangle, such as a scalene, right, equilateral, etc.

Unpacking Your learning Targets
Standard # - _Bio.2.2.1_

Standard 3 – Infer how human activities (including population growth, pollution, global warming, burning of fossil fuels, habitat destruction and introduction of nonnative species) may impact the environment.

Standard Deconstruction - Read anchor Standard - Read your grade level standard - Reduce your standard to essential word

(Infer) how human activities may impact the environment

including population growth, pollution, (global warming,) burning of fossil fuels, habitat destruction and introduction of nonnative species

Word Wise - Examine the key words and phrases in the standard. What word(s) do you want to pullout for discussion and/or clarification – Look up and define chosen word(s).

Infer – to derive by reasoning; conclude or judge from premises or evidence

Global Warming – An increase in the earth's average atmospheric temperature that causes corresponding changes in climate and that may result from the greenhouse effect

Figure 6.4 Bio.2.2.1 Word Wise

Figure 6.4 provides an example from the Biology standard; here I selected two terms : "infer" and "global warming". The use of "infer" in this standard provides a weighted significance to the standard while also specifically dictating what the students must be able to do.

In order to properly infer, one must be able to go back to the evidence and explain their reasoning for their conclusion or opinion. This is an important component of this standard because it informs the teacher that students must be able to justify their thoughts and conclusions with evidence. This standard does not cite that students must arrive at a specific conclusion, and therefore the inference one student makes may be different from another.

Global warming was selected due not only to its role in the standard, but also for its potential to be easily misinterpreted or misrepresented. The definition for global warming clearly states " … changes in climate … that may result from the greenhouse effect". The word "may" means to express a possibility; it is not an absolute in terms of "it does" or "it does not" or "yes/no". Educators must be sure to give students an opportunity to use their higher order thinking skills to analyze and evaluate a variety of information in order to arrive at their own conclusions through logical inferences. Do not rob your students of these fantastic learning opportunities because you have already prescribed to your own inferences, thoughts, and/or beliefs.

Conclusion

If you were working along with one of the same standards, did you select more words or something different? If so that's okay; different words or phrases may carry more weight or need additional clarification for different people. As such, if you are currently or may eventually be working through this process with a team, don't feel like you should all have selected the same word(s). A deeper and more thorough understanding of the standard(s) will occur through collaboration. Just because one person believes a word to be potentially significant and their teammate does not share the same initial interpretation, does not make it wrong. It is through an open and honest dialog after each part of this process that you will begin to simultaneously deepen and align your understanding of your standards.

Work Cited

Evans, V. (2017). Why english is such a difficult language to learn: Reasons that second language learners find english tough to master. Retrieved from www.psychologytoday.com/us/blog/language-in-the-mind/201702/why-english-is-such-difficult-language-learn

Cut the Fluff

Introduction

When you read a standard you need to interpret it as a call to action. The basis of any standard is, in and of itself, a directive for learning, and the standards that make up any particular instructional unit need to be viewed as the map that guides you into your instructional foray. This part of the process does not focus on what the teacher must do, we'll get to that later: rather it helps the educator identify specifically what the student(s) must do.

The importance of focusing on what the student(s) must do, prior to focusing on any of the instructional components, allows us to place a laser-like focus precisely on the desired student outcome(s). It is, after all, a student's ability to demonstrate proficiency of the targeted learning outcome that will indicate how successful the instructional was.

This part of the process helps educators to focus on the basic premise of the chosen standard by reconstructing the essential words and phrases. The focus here remains specifically on what the students need to be able to do in a simple and easy to understand manner.

Sum It Up

Our goal for this section is to Cut the Fluff by condensing and/or reorganizing the chosen standard to make it easier to mentally digest. Therefore, if you find yourself using more words than the original standard you should probably revisit your work.

Most standards tend to be pretty lean to begin with and there usually isn't a lot of unnecessary wording, or fluff, to be cut out. However, in this part of the unpacking process you're not simply summarizing a standard; you are condensing it to just the action that the student needs to be able to complete. By drawing the focus specifically to the action(s) that the students need to complete, we will be able to better plan lessons, activities, and tasks that align directly to the desired student outcome(s), and then later we will revisit this part of the process order to assist in the formation of the corresponding learning targets.

Step One

As with all the previous examples, and examples to come, I will be utilizing the 3rd grade reading standard to walk through the steps and then provide you with the completed examples from 7th grade math and high school biology at the end of the chapter.

Begin by re-reading your standard, listed below.

Standard – "Ask and answer questions to demonstrate understanding of a text, referring explicitly to the text as the basis for the answers."

Standard Reduction – "Ask and answer questions ... demonstrate understanding of a text ... referring explicitly to the text"

Work Along
Re-read your standard, and then re-read your key words and phrases from the Standard Deconstruction

Step Two

The second step in this part of the process is to identify the student action(s) from the essential words and phrases. Remember that you are not identifying "how" they must demonstrate their proficiency of the standard; rather you are just pulling out "what" they must do. In this case the students must be able to "demonstrate".

Now dig a little deeper and we see that student must be able to "demonstrate understanding of a text". This is "what" the student must be able to do in order to show proficiency for the given standard.

> **Work Along**
>
> From the standard identify "what" the students must do; this is the specific action(s) that the standard is dictating the students must be able to complete. Stay focused on the action words/verbs such as recognize, demonstrate, apply, ask, compare, explain (see Figure 4.2 for more examples)
>
> You can choose to circle, underline, or highlight the identified student action(s).

Step Three

You just identified the student outcome(s), or "what" the student must do; now you need to identify "how" the student must do it. At times you will find that the directions a standard gives for "how" something must be done may be split up within the standard and not in one clean sequence. Many standards involve students demonstrating multiple ways to achieve an objective, or the approach they need to master may be multifaceted.

Regardless of how many layers there are to "how" a student must demonstrate the specified outcome(s), it is important to identify and simplify these. Doing this will assist both you and your colleagues with gaining a deeper and cleaner understanding of the standard.

> **Work Along**
>
> Identify "how" the standard is directing students to complete the specific action(s). Stay focused on just the specific actions and nothing else. Think of it in terms of students will demonstrate the indicated tack by doing ____.
>
> You can choose to circle, underline, or highlight the identified student action(s).

Step Four

The final step at this stage of the unpacking process is to rework/reword the "what" and "how" you just identified from the standard into a simplified statement. You can do this most easily by ensuring that the "what" and "how" remain separated and are not overlapping each other. Do this by first stating "what" the student is supposed to do and then state "how" they are supposed to do it, or vice-versa. Avoid stating the "how" then the "what" then the "how" again; this will only leave room for confusion later.

> **Work Along**
>
> Write down "what" the students must do, then write down "how" the students must do it; insert transitional words if necessary to form a single coherent statement

 ## Examples

In the examples on the following pages you can see how the essential words and phrases that were identified in the previous step compose both what a student is supposed to do and how they are supposed to do it. Each example is demonstrated as a stand-alone example so you can clearly see each standard.

When examining standard RI3.1, in Figure 7.1, we first identify "what" students must be able to do. Students must be able to "demonstrate understanding of a text". We then examine "how" they must demonstrate their understanding of a text; the standard informs us that students must "ask and answer questions … referring explicitly to the text".

Cut the Fluff

Unpacking Your learning Targets
Standard # - __RI3.1__

Standard 1 – Ask and answer questions to demonstrate understanding of a text, referring explicitly to the text as the basis for the answers.

Standard Deconstruction: Read your chosen standard and reduce it to just its essential words/ phrases.

(Ask and answer questions)   (demonstrate understanding of a text)   (referring explicitly to the text)

Punctuation Pitfalls: Reread your standard - Consider all the punctuation signs and/or conjunctions - Think about how it effects your understanding of the standard - Share your thinking with a partner

The comma after "text," provides an emphasis to separate what the students need to do from how they will need to do it, but it does not necessarily have the influence to impact ones understanding of the standard

Word Wise: Examine the key words and phrases in the standard. What word(s) do you want to pullout for discussion and/or clarification – Look up and define chosen word(s).

 Explicitly – Fully and clearly expressed or demonstrated; leaving nothing merely implied; unequivocal

Cut the Fluff: Reread your grade level standard. Condense and summarize the standard (what do the students need to be able to do, and how)

  What - demonstrate understanding of a text
  How - by asking and answering questions that refer explicitly to the text

Figure 7.1 RI3.1 Cut the Fluff

In Figure 7.2, differentiating between the "what" and "how" in our 7th grade Math standard is not quite as clear as the 3rd grade reading standard, in the previous example. When examining "what" students must do we can easily determine that they must "draw," but they are not just doing a free draw; students must draw "geometric shapes" or "construct triangles" and they must be able to "notice when given conditions determine a unique triangle, more than one triangle, or no triangle".

However, none of the quoted words or statements above tell us "how" these things are to be done. How are students supposed to be able to draw? Students are to draw "freehand, with a ruler, and with technology". How are students supposed to draw their triangles? And

Cut the Fluff

Unpacking Your learning Targets
Standard # - __7G.A.2__

Standard 2 - Draw (freehand, with a ruler and protractor, and with technology) geometric shapes with given conditions. Focus on constructing triangles from three measures of angles or sides, noticing when the conditions determine a unique triangle, more than one triangle, or no triangle.

Standard Deconstruction: Read your chosen standard and reduce it to just its essential words/ phrases.

(Draw)   (free hand, with a ruler and protractor, and with technology)
(geometric shapes with given conditions) (Constructing triangles from three measures of angles or sides)
(determine a unique triangle, more than one triangle, or no triangle)

Word Wise: Examine the key words and phrases in the standard. What word(s) do you want to pullout for discussion and/or clarification – Look up and define chosen word(s).

Unique Triangle – A triangle that can only be drawn one way. If a triangle is not unique then more than one triangle can be formed using the same measures.

Cut the Fluff: Reread your grade level standard. Condense and summarize the standard (what do the students need to be able to do, and how)

What - Draw geometric shapes, construct triangles, notice when given conditions determine a unique triangle, more than one triangle, or no triangle.

How – Free hand, with a ruler, and with technology from three measures of angles or sides

Figure 7.2 7G.A.2 Cut the Fluff

how are they supposed to recognize when "given conditions determine a unique triangle, more than one triangle, or no triangle"? This is answered by the statement "from three measures of angles or sides". When rereading the standard you can see that it mentions "given conditions" in the first sentence and then defines the "given conditions" in the second sentence as "three measures of angles or sides".

Differentiating between what students are supposed to do and how they are supposed to do it in the Biology standard in Figure 7.3 represents a prime example of how standards will often be written with intermixed "what's" and "how's". The original composition of this standard starts with what a student is supposed to do, then it roughly injects how they are supposed to do it, before ending with the rest of the "what".

Unpacking Your learning Targets
Standard # - Bio.2.2.1

Standard 3 – Infer how human activities (including population growth, pollution, global warming, burning of fossil fuels, habitat destruction and introduction of nonnative species) may impact the environment.

Standard Deconstruction: Read anchor Standard - Read your grade level standard - Reduce your standard to essential word

Infer how human activities may impact the environment

including population growth, pollution, global warming, burning of fossil fuels, habitat destruction and introduction of nonnative species

Word Wise: Examine the key words and phrases in the standard. What word(s) do you want to pullout for discussion and/or clarification – Look up and define chosen word(s).

Infer – to derive by reasoning; conclude or judge from premises or evidence

https://www.dictionary.com/browse/infer?s=t

Global Warming – An increase in the earth's average atmospheric temperature that causes corresponding changes in climate and that may result from the greenhouse effect

Cut the Fluff: Reread your grade level standard. Condense and summarize the standard (what do the students need to be able to do, and how)

  What – Infer how human activities may impact the environment

  How – including population growth, pollution, global warming, burning of fossil fuels, habitat destruction and introduction of nonnative species

Figure 7.3 Bio. 2.2.1 Cut the Fluff

"Infer how human activities ... may impact the environment" represents the combined "what". Hopefully you find this fairly straightforward. "including population growth, pollution, global warming, burning fossil fuels, habitat destruction and introduction of non-native species" identifies how students are supposed to accomplish the "what". However, this standard is unique because it does not identify an operative word or phrase with the "how"; instead it is left open to the teacher to determine how they will integrate these things in order to assist students in their inferences.

Cut the Fluff

 Conclusion

Standards are inherently designed to dictate student outcomes; it is then the teacher's role to design lesson plans in order to facilitate the progress toward and eventual proficiency/mastery of these outcomes. By focusing specifically on what students are supposed to do and how they are supposed to do it, teachers will be able to better progress though their instructional planning process.

Sometimes the standards can be easily dissected and the what and how are clearly indicated; other times the standards can be clouded with ambiguity. The important aspect from this step in the process is to pull everything to a student-first frame of mind. After completing this step you should begin asking yourself questions such as "what do my students need to be able to do?", "How can I best assist my students to gain this knowledge and learn these skills?", and "What do my students already know that will help them reach proficiency on their grade level standards?"

# Standard Reconstruction

Introduction

Standard reconstruction is a culminating step that allows the educator(s) to bring all their previous work together in order to rephrase, simplify, and clarify a standard in student-friendly language. The completion of this step highlights many advantages of the unpacking process. Not only does the completion of Standard Reconstruction covey a clear understanding of a given standard from the teacher or team that has done the unpacking, but it also allows the standard to be more easily digested in the future, especially for those that didn't have a direct hand in unpacking it. In addition to aiding those who will be working directly with the standard as part of their curriculum, it also allows the standard to be conveyed in a manner that can be more easily understood by students, parents, and other teachers that may not share the same content, but are trying to incorporate cross curricular tasks/activities.

Add Story About Teachers That Post Unaltered Standards on Their Board

Use Your Words

I'm sure most of us have heard the saying "use your words" as it is a common redirection for toddlers that may be in the midst of a temper

Standard Reconstruction

tantrum or are having trouble expressing themselves. Parents use this saying in hopes that it will give the child an opportunity to pause and think about what they want to say before just speaking incoherently or nonsensically. The saying can also be used good-naturedly between adults when someone gets overly excited and forgets to provide sufficient context or details and leaves their friend with that uncomprehending stare, that can commonly be followed by "Okay Sean, I know you're excited, but I really need you to slow down and use your words." Although this is usually followed by a casual expletive and a smile, the point remains that in order to appropriately communicate either verbally or through the written word, one needs to ensure that their message is clear and concise.

Before explaining the steps involved in Standard Reduction it is imperative that we recognize the purpose of this step. The objective here is not to demonstrate one's mastery of old English or to promote our Shakespearian inner self. Thou hasn't but need to identify said hindrance to the written ambiguity in order to find the quintessence of the implied objective(s) in order to reveal the core synergies that formulate the rudimentary tasks that our scholars must be embodied with. Blah! In other words – the purpose of Standard Reduction is to simplify and clarify the intent of the standard.

Step One

Begin by re-reading the "what" and "how" from the previous step, Cut the Fluff. Now make a mental note of what makes more sense to begin the sentence with – the "what" or the "how". In truth it may not always matter and may be more personal feng shui. However, just like the previous step, we want to ensure that the "what" and "how" remain separated and do not overlap each other.

Work Along

Re-read the final product from Cut the Fluff; decide if it makes more sense to start the sentence with the "what" or the "how"

Step Two

Using any needed transitional words, revise the "what" and "how" statements in order to form a clear and coherent sentence. Depending on the length of the standard you may need to use multiple sentences in order to properly capture everything. Preferably, the reconstructed standard should always be shorter than the original, but there will be times when it is approximately the same length.

> **Work Along**
> Combine the "what" and "how" using the appropriate transitions

 ## Examples

In the examples on the following pages, you can see how easily one can reconstruct any given standard after going through the steps to fully immerse themselves in it. Separating exactly what a student is supposed to do and how they are supposed to do it provides the easiest context from which to proceed into this step.

In this first example, in Figure 8.1, there is actually very little that needs to be changed in the reading standard. I started this Standard Reconstruction by stating what the students are supposed to do: "Demonstrate understanding of a text". I generally prefer to start with "What students are supposed to do" as I believe it to be a more linear way of thinking. I then added "by asking and answering questions that refer to the text". The astute readers may have noticed that I omitted the word "explicitly", even though I made certain to highlight this word from the Word Wise section. Now before you cry foul, ask yourself what is the difference in the meaning of the following three statements?

1) ask and answer questions that refer to the text
2) ask and answer questions that refer explicitly to the text
3) ask and answer questions that refer explicitly to the text and nothing else

Standard Reconstruction

What, if anything, would you have students do differently in order to complete any of these tasks? The answer is nothing; all three of these statements mean exactly the same thing, only with added emphasis. Regardless of the added emphasis, a teacher's lesson plan would utilize the same tasks and activities to complete them.

Unpacking Your learning Targets
Standard # - __RI3.1__

Standard 1 – Ask and answer questions to demonstrate understanding of a text, referring explicitly to the text as the basis for the answers.

Standard Deconstruction: Read your chosen standard and reduce it to just its essential words/ phrases.

Ask and answer questions demonstrate understanding of a text referring explicitly to the text

Punctuation Pitfalls: Reread your standard - Consider all the punctuation signs and/or conjunctions- Think about how it effects your understanding of the standard - Share your thinking with a partner

The comma after "text," provides an emphasis to separate what the students need to do from how they will need to do it, but it does not necessarily have the influence to impact ones understanding of the standard

Word Wise: Examine the key words and phrases in the standard. What word(s) do you want to pullout for discussion and/or clarification – Look up and define chosen word(s).

Explicitly – Fully and clearly expressed or demonstrated; leaving nothing merely implied; unequivocal

Cut the Fluff: Reread your grade level standard. Condense and summarize the standard (what do the students need to be able to do, and how)

    What - demonstrate understanding of a text

    How - by asking and answering questions that refer explicitly to the text

Standard Reconstruction: Focusing on what your students are supposed to do and how they are supposed to do it write an explanation and/ or paraphrase the standard in your own words.

Demonstrate understanding of a text by asking and answering questions that refer to the text

Figure 8.1 RI3.1 Standard Reconstruction

I generally enjoy reconstructing standards like 7G.A.2 because they are inherently messy. The original author(s) of the standard intermixed the "what's" and the "how" into the same sentence, and although there are opportunities to clarify the original standard there is also very little that can be cut out; in instances such as this you need to be careful not to expand the standard or make it unnecessarily wordy.

Standard Reconstruction

Unpacking Your learning Targets
Standard # - __7G.A.2__

Standard 2 - Draw (freehand, with a ruler and protractor, and with technology) geometric shapes with given conditions. Focus on constructing triangles from three measures of angles or sides, noticing when the conditions determine a unique triangle, more than one triangle, or no triangle.

Standard Deconstruction: Read your chosen standard and reduce it to just its essential words/ phrases.

Draw free hand, with a ruler and protractor, and with technology geometric shapes with given conditions Constructing triangles from three measures of angles or sides determine a unique triangle, more than one triangle, or no triangle

Word Wise: Examine the key words and phrases in the standard. What word(s) do you want to pullout for discussion and/or clarification – Look up and define chosen word(s).

Unique Triangle – A triangle that can only be drawn one way. If a triangle is not unique then more than one triangle can be formed using the same measures.

Cut the Fluff: Reread your grade level standard. Condense and summarize the standard (what do the students need to be able to do, and how)

What - Draw geometric shapes, construct triangles, notice when given conditions determine a unique triangle, more than one triangle, or no triangle.

How – Free hand, with a ruler, and with technology from three measures of angles or sides

Standard Reconstruction: Focusing on what your students are supposed to do and how they are supposed to do it write an explanation and/ or paraphrase the standard in your own words.

Draw geometric shapes, focusing on triangles and identifying when given conditions determine a unique triangle, more than one triangle, or no triangle. Construct the shapes from three given measures of angles or sides, drawing them free hand, with a ruler, and with technology.

Figure 8.2 7G.A.2 Standard Reconstruction

As you can see in Figure 8.2, I chose to start by stating what the students are supposed to do: "Draw geometric shapes". I added the word "focusing" because, just like the original standard, it adds clarification as to what geometric shapes should receive the most attention. I then ended this first sentence with "identifying when given conditions …" This final part is far too important to omit because it clearly dictates three objectives which we will end up turning into separate learning targets.

The second sentence articulates two directives for how students are supposed to complete the aforementioned tasks. The first is that students need to "construct the shapes from three given measures of angles or

Standard Reconstruction

sides," and the second dictates that the shapes are to be drawn "free hand, with a ruler, and with technology."

Although we were not able to notably shorten this standard, we were able to add clarity by reorganizing and rewording it so that it flows more logically.

This biology standard in Figure 8.3 provides a good example of a Standard Reconstruction with a multitude of possible reconstructions.

Unpacking Your learning Targets
Standard # - Bio.2.2.1

Standard 3 – Infer how human activities (including population growth, pollution, global warming, burning of fossil fuels, habitat destruction and introduction of nonnative species) may impact the environment.

Standard Deconstruction: Read anchor Standard - Read your grade level standard - Reduce your standard to essential word

Infer how human activities may impact the environment

including population growth, pollution, global warming, burning of fossil fuels, habitat destruction and

introduction of nonnative species

Word Wise: Examine the key words and phrases in the standard. What word(s) do you want to pullout for discussion and/or clarification – Look up and define chosen word(s).

Infer – to derive by reasoning; conclude or judge from premises or evidence

Global Warming – An increase in the earth's average atmospheric temperature that causes corresponding changes in climate and that may result from the greenhouse effect

Cut the Fluff: Reread your grade level standard. Condense and summarize the standard (what do the students need to be able to do, and how)

    What – Infer how human activities may impact the environment

    How – including population growth, pollution, global warming, burning of fossil fuels, habitat destruction and introduction of nonnative species

Standard Reconstruction: Focusing on what your students are supposed to do and how they are supposed to do it write an explanation and/ or paraphrase the standard in your own words.

Infer how human activities may impact the environment paying special attention to population growth, pollution, global warming, burning fossil fuels, habitat deconstruction, and the introduction of nonnative species.

Figure 8.3 Bio.2.2.1 Standard Reconstruction

Generally the reconstruction process leaves room for subjectivity with the use of transitional words, placement of the "How" and the "What", and/or punctuation (weather to split something up into multiple sentences or leave it as one. In the example in Figure 7.3 I chose to leave the standard in one sentence, simply adding the transitionary words "paying special attention to"; however it could easily be broken up into two sentences similar to the example below.

> *Infer how human activities may impact the environment. Include population growth, pollution, global warming, burning fossil fuels, habitat deconstruction, and the introduction of non-native species.*

This standard is also straightforward enough that one could easily justify leaving the "What" and the "How" intermixed.

> *Infer how human activities such as population growth, pollution, global warming, burning fossil fuels, habitat deconstruction, and the introduction of non-native species may impact the environment.*

In my experiences I prefer to separate the "What" and "How" in order to provide greater clarity, simplification, and consistency across all standards, but this is not a requirement.

All of these options are correct, so when you get to this step in the process please understand that, just like driving from point A to point B, there is more than one way to get to your final destination.

Conclusion

Standard Reconstruction is a simple and straightforward process because you have the advantage of pulling from the work you already did in the previous four steps. If you work through this process with a team it is likely that the final product will differ slightly from one group/person to the next. Remember that this is perfectly normal and it is highly probable that everyone achieved the goal of simplifying and clarifying the chosen standard.

Usually most individuals or teams that embark on the process of unpacking their standards would be done now. After all, we literally just covered and worked through the process of unpacking your standards.

Standard Reconstruction

However, stopping here would leave a large gap in ensuring that the unpacking process was done in a way that will lead to strengthening classroom instruction and bring greater consistency across a grade level or content area. This is why we are rebranding the process of unpacking your standards to unpacking your learning targets.

9 | With Higher Order Thinking in Mind

Introduction

In the preceding chapters we have gone through the basic process of unpacking a standard, leaving only the final step of writing the corresponding learning targets. But before we move to the final step, we must *refamiliarize* ourselves with critical components needed to write high quality scaffolded learning targets. I intentionally used the word refamiliarize, because I am confident in the assumption that nearly every practicing educator has either used or has at least heard of either Bloom's Taxonomy or Webb's Depth of Knowledge (DOK). There are, of course, other models that represent higher order thinking models, including Marzano's New Taxonomy and Briggs and Collis's SOLO Taxonomy. And these taxonomies could just as easily be used to facilitate the writing of scaffolded learning targets. However, I am going to focus only on works and adaptations by Bloom and Webb, as these are the two that seem to be the most prevalent in my experiences.

Both Bloom's and Webb's cognitive thinking models serve as frameworks for articulating and planning multiple aspects of teaching and learning, including, but not limited to learning objectives, lessons, assessments, alignment to learning objectives questions and activities so that students may best approach their learning.

It is for these reasons that I originally began intentionally incorporating higher order thinking skills into learning targets and why I think that you will also find this pairing both beneficial and undeniably logical. Research has long indicated that Higher Order thinking skills allow students to learn and understand concepts holistically while promoting reflective learning and meta-cognitive abilities and traits (Shukla & Dungsungnoen, 2016). It has also been shown that teaching strategies that align to Higher Order thinking skills can lead to increased meta-cognition (Anderson & Krathwohl, 2001; Roberts & Erdos, 1993) and the integration of differentiated instruction (Anderson & Krathwohl, 2001). Research also indicates that the integration of scaffolded thinking routines can build student capacity and commitment toward thinking (Ritchhart, 2002; Ritchhart et al., 2006).

Whether or not you intentionally incorporate higher order thinking skills into your lessons, they will usually align to one of the cognitive levels, even if the alignment is completely haphazard. However, it is the intentionality of the alignment that will help ensure that the instruction is appropriately scaffolded and that the lessons foster greater student outcomes.

The general learning process aligned to Bloom's taxonomy suggests that

- Before you can **understand** a concept, you must **remember** it.
- To **apply** a concept you must first **understand** it.
- In order to **analyze** something you must first be able to **apply** it.
- Before you can evaluate the impact you must have analyzed it.
- Before you can **create** you must have **remembered, understood, applied, analyzed, and evaluated**.

This does not mean that information must always be sequenced in this manner as learning can start at any point, but inherent learning is going to occur in the beginning stages. When introducing material that is brand-new it is important that students first build a foundational base of knowledge before moving to the higher levels (Anderson & Krathwohl, 2001; Churches, 2009; Shabatu, 2018).

Origins and Evolutions of Bloom's Taxonomy

In collaboration with some of his colleagues, Benjamin Bloom published the Taxonomy of Educational Objectives; this became commonly known as Bloom's Taxonomy. The framework created by Bloom consisted of six major categories (knowledge, comprehension, application, analysis, synthesis, and evaluation). Since it was first released in 1956, Bloom's Taxonomy has been widely used by educators for a multitude of reasons, but upon its release it was meant to be used to classify learning outcomes and objectives. Bloom (1956) provided brief overviews of his classification system in the appendix of his Taxonomy of Educational Objectives (pp. 201–207) stating that

Knowledge – involves the recall of specifics, methods, processes, patterns, structures, or settings

Comprehension – is the understanding of what is being communicated but without the need to relate to other material or understand its full implications

Application – is the use of concepts, notions, and thoughts in specific situations

Analysis – is the ability to break down a communication to its fundamental elements in order to establish an explicit understanding of the structural and organizational relationships within

Synthesis – involves putting together elements and parts to form a complete picture/product that was not clearly visible before

Evaluation – is making sound judgements about the value of material and methods for given purposes

The original sequence of cognitive skills in Bloom's taxonomy was later revised in 2001 by Lorin Anderson and David Krathwohl in order to expand potentially static perceptions of the educational objectives first proposed in Bloom's original work. The Revised Taxonomy uses verbs and gerunds (adding "ing" to a noun in order to express it as an action) in order to describe the cognitive processes that individuals will approach and work with their knowledge. Iowa State University, Center for Excellence in Learning and Teaching, 2019)

Remember – Retrieve relevant knowledge and/or information
Understand – Construct meaning from instructional messages, including oral, written, and graphic communication

Apply – Carry out or use a procedure in a given situation
Analyze – Distinguish between different parts
Evaluate – Make judgements based on criteria and standards
Create – Put elements together to form a coherent whole; reorganize into a new pattern or structure

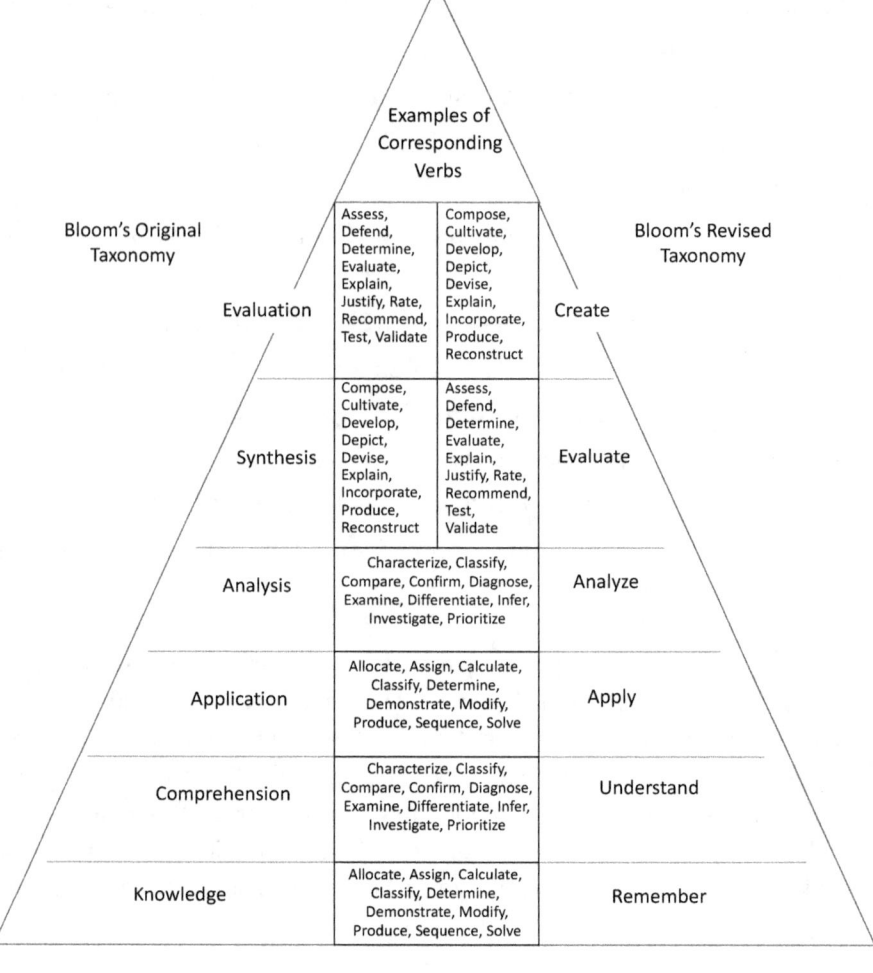

Figure 9.1 Comparison of Bloom's Taxonomy and Bloom's Revised Taxonomy

With Higher Order Thinking in Mind

The side-by-side comparison of Bloom's original taxonomy and the revised taxonomy in Figure 9.1 show the progression from lower order thinking skills to higher order thinking skills. The idea behind this is that each of the domains build upon each other and that in order to demonstrate an understanding of something you must first have knowledge of the topic to draw from, and in order to apply this knowledge you must first be able to demonstrate an understanding of it and so on, and so forth.

Bloom's taxonomy evolved yet again in 2009 when Andrew Churches utilized the revised version to create a version of the taxonomy geared for the digital age. Commonly referred to as Bloom's Digital Taxonomy, Churches stayed true to focusing on the cognitive thinking skills through actionable learning activities that prioritize the uses of technology.

There is no doubt that Bloom's taxonomy will continue to evolve, and regardless of which version you prefer, the progression of the lower order thinking skills to the higher order thinking skills remains mostly the same, with the key differences being in the actionable teaching/learning activities. There is no reason to adhere to a single version/rendition of Bloom's Taxonomy; instead utilize the various adaptations to deepen your understanding and facilitate incorporating Bloom's taxonomy into your instructional planning.

Each level of Bloom's Taxonomy is summarized below, with the intent of capturing key aspects from both the work of Anderson and Krathwohl (2001) and Andrew Church (2009). Following each level there are examples of potential instructional activities that align with each level of the hierarchy. Although the examples of instructional activities provided can be used to help direct practical application, they in no way constitute an exhaustive list; they are merely a sampling.

Remember(ing) – The lowest level of Bloom's Taxonomy, but it is also the foundational layer that all cognitive skills build upon. Retrieving knowledge can be used to produce definitions and lists, recalling information and demonstrating how to access information. Drawing from both the 2001 Revised Taxonomy and the 2009 Digital Taxonomy, demonstrating acquisition of this cognitive skill is not limited only to remembering/recalling information, but also the knowledge of how to retrieve the desired information. McNulty (2017) states that the active task of retrieving information, especially when so much is available, is a building block to be used in all the other cognitive levels.

> Aligned task/activities starters
> Make a list of the characters in the story.
> Which is true or false?
> What does it mean to _____?
> Turn to your partner and share what you know about _____?
> Using your laptop, what facts can you find on/about _____?

Understand(ing) – Bloom (1956) originally categorized the second level of his hierarchy as comprehension and stated that it represents the lowest level of understating. Here students can demonstrate an understanding or appreciation of something through a discussion, and generalization. Students can also organize information that they have gathered/researched and identify connections/links between various resources while constructing meaning and relevance from the organizational process (McNulty, 2017).

> Aligned task/activities starters
> Re-tell the story in your own words
> Create a timeline to illustrate the sequence of events
> What is the main idea of passage?
> Explain how you solved the problem
> What are the differences between _____ and _____?

Apply(ing) – Logically placed after *Understanding*, the organizational structure of Bloom's Taxonomy suggests that students must understand something before they can apply it. At this level students will apply their acquired knowledge/skills to either the execution or implementation of a problem or procedure, or in a given situation. Heick (2019) provides some brief possible example activities at the Application level in order to establish easily transferable relevance to classroom tasks and activities. Although it is understood that there are a number of ways that students can apply their knowledge to actual situations, he suggests that students could utilize a formula to solve a problem, or students could reconstruct the passage of a new law through a given government/system.

Aligned task/activities starters
Using Pythagoras's theorem solve the following problem.
Develop a series of instructions in order to _____?
Classify the following items into _____ categories.

Analyze(ing) – The level where the students learn to process data by breaking down objects or ideas into smaller/simpler parts. This is done so that a relevant order or hierarchy of thoughts and ideas can be made clear and relationships between the parts can be easily identified (Bloom, 1956).

Aligned task/activities starters
What is the underlying theme of the story?
What are some of the unintended consequences of _____?
Examine the data from _____, what information are you able to gather?
After examining the given information, explain how different parts of a process work together.
Compare and contrast _____.

Evaluate(ing) – This level requires students to make criteria-based judgements through the processes of critiquing and checking (McNulty, 2017). The focus of the evaluation process should determine if a student can justify a stance, decision, method, or opinion. The educational environment provides a multitude of opportunities for discussions, debates, and determinations. Possible activities for this could include defending a particular stance or opinion on something with factual and/or logical reasoning, making determinations on the credibility of sources, interpreting the significance or implications of a new invention or technological advancement, or justifying and/or explaining a particular thought process used to solve a problem.

Aligned task/activities starters
What would happen if_____?
What are the strengths and weaknesses of the current plan to_____?
Justify your thinking on _____.
Evaluate your research materials; are your sources credible? Why or why not?
Why did the author choose to _____?

Create(ing) – The final level in Bloom's Revised Taxonomy is focused on combining elements together in order to form a new product or to create alternative solutions. This level draws on all the levels before it by necessitating that students can remember and understand the knowledge while also being able to apply and analyze it prior to evaluating various outcome(s) and process(es) to generate or produce a new product. Just like the other levels the educational landscape is rich with opportunities that teachers can use to facilitate this level. Students could create their own problem sets, work on solutions to various local and/or global issues/problems, or write a story or poem based on set criteria.

> Aligned task/activities starters
> Create a video clip to introduce the idea or solution you created to _____?
> Construct a viable alternative to _____.
> Frame a counter-argument for _____.
> Write a four-stanza poem using at least two analogies.
> Create a word problem that requires the use of a linear equation to solve.

Bloom's Taxonomy may be old news to many, but its practical applications continue to influence the modern classroom, providing educators with a scaffolded way to think about teaching and learning, increase rigor, plan assignments, frame discussions, create assessments, ensure instructional alignment, and to clarify learning objectives/goals (Armstrong, 2019).

Origins and Development of Webb's Depth of Knowledge

In 1997 Norman Webb developed a progression of measures for the purpose of systematically analyzing the alignment between standards and standardized assessments and to serve as a tool to increase the cognitive complexity of such assessments. Webb based his model on the assumption that curricular elements can all be categorized according to the cognitive demands required to complete them.

With Higher Order Thinking in Mind

Each level in his depth of knowledge (DOK) reflects a different level of cognitive demands/expectations. For this reason the process that Webb created also demonstrated a high aptitude for reviewing curricular alignment.

Webb (2002) delineated his depth of knowledge into four levels. Although the specific titles of each level slightly change in different content areas; the instructional focus remains the same. The chart below provides an adapted overview of each DOK level and their instructional focus.

Similar to Bloom's Taxonomy, the DOK level is meant to reflect the *complexity* of the cognitive process need to complete a task, not its *difficulty*. The DOK level describes the kind of thinking required by a task and is not a dictate of whether or not a task is difficult. Figure 9.2 below provides a snapshot of Webb's Depth of Knowledge.

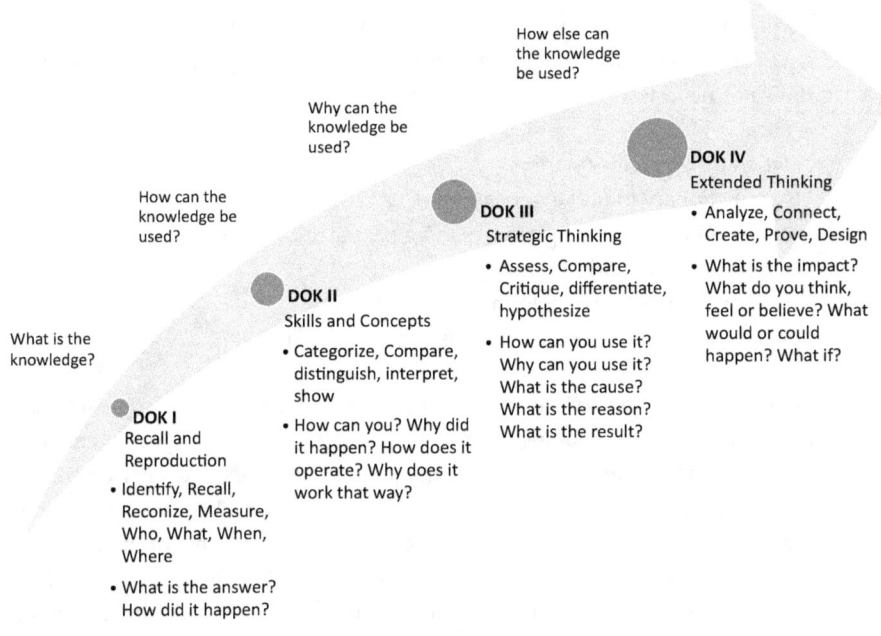

Figure 9.2 Webb's Depth of Knowledge

A more detailed look into Webb's Depth of Knowledge through the combined work by Mississippi State University and the Mississippi Department of Education (2009) shows each level of Norman Webb's DOK is summarized to be applicable across the content areas. These summarizations are provided below, along with some of Webb's (2002) content-specific examples, to represent potential instructional activities that align with each DOK level. Although the examples of instructional activities provided can be used to help direct practical application, they in no way constitute an exhaustive list, they are merely a sampling.

DOK 1 – Recall and Reproduction: Curricular elements that fall into this category involve basic tasks that require students to recall or reproduce knowledge and/or skills. The subject matter content at this particular level usually involves working with facts, terms and/or properties of objects. It may also involve use of simple procedures and/or formulas. There is little transformation or extended processing of the target knowledge required by the tasks that fall into this category. Key words that often denote this particular level include: list, identify and define. A student answering a Level 1 item either knows the answer or does not; that is, the answer does not need to be "figured out" or "solved."

Aligned task/activities starters
Use a dictionary to find the meaning of words.
Identify figurative language in a reading passage.
Use punctuation marks correctly.
Recall or recognize a fact, term, or property.
Perform a routine procedure such as measuring length.

DOK 2 – Skills and Concepts: Includes the engagement of some mental processing beyond recalling or reproducing a response. This level generally requires students to contrast or compare people, places, events and concepts; convert information from one form to another; classify or sort items into meaningful categories; describe or explain issues and problems, patterns, cause and effect, significance or impact, relationships, points of view or processes. A Level 2 "describe or explain" would require students to go beyond a description or explanation of recalled information to describe or explain a result or "how" or "why." The learner should make use of information in a context different from the one in which it was learned.

DOK 2 Aligned task/activities starters
Use context cues to identify the meaning of unfamiliar words
Predict a logical outcome based on information in a reading selection
Construct compound sentences.
Specify and explain the relationship between facts, terms, properties, or variables.
Organize, represent and interpret data.

DOK 3 – Strategic Thinking: Items falling into this category demand a short-term use of higher order thinking processes, such as analysis and evaluation, to solve real-world problems with predictable outcomes. Stating one's reasoning is a key marker of tasks that fall into this particular category. The expectation established for tasks at this level tends to require coordination of knowledge and skill from multiple subject-matter areas to carry out processes and reach a solution in a project-based setting. Key processes that often denote this particular level include: analyze, explain and support with evidence, generalize, and create.

DOK 3 Aligned task/activities starters
Summarize information from multiple sources to address a specific topic
Cite evidence and develop a logical argument
Draw conclusions from observations
Solve non-routine problems
Form conclusions from experimental data.

DOK 4 – Extended Thinking: Curricular elements assigned to this level demand extended use of higher order thinking processes such as synthesis, reflection, assessment and adjustment of plans over time. Students are engaged in conducting investigations to solve real-world problems with unpredictable outcomes. Employing and sustaining strategic thinking processes over a longer period of time to solve the problem is a key feature of curricular objectives that are assigned to this level. Key strategic thinking processes that denote this particular level include: synthesize, reflect, conduct, and manage.

DOK 4 Aligned task/activities starters
Examine and explain alternative perspectives across a variety of sources
Analyze and synthesize information from multiple sources

Write an analysis of two selections, identifying the common theme and generating a purpose that is appropriate for making connections between a finding and related concepts and phenomena.

Conduct an investigation, from specifying a problem to designing and carrying out an experiment, to analyzing its data and forming conclusions.

 ## Conclusion

Although there is a lot of information out there that speaks to the values and advantages of integrating higher order thinking skills into your professional tool kit, it cannot be overstated how critical the role of the teacher is when it comes to incorporating higher order thinking skills into one's instructional planning and their learning targets. Teaching higher order thinking skills requires time, persistence, and intentionality. Jere Brophy (1992) emphasizes that properly utilizing higher order thinking in one's instructions requires commitment to class discussion, debate and problem solving, all of which take time and intentionality.

Teaching with higher order thinking in mind involves either strategically fostering or ensuring the existence of foundational knowledge, and then introducing conceptual scaffolds and challenges to build upon that knowledge. However, the ongoing regurgitation of facts and processes will not naturally facilitate an interactive discourse during lessons and activities and composes the lower levels of Bloom's and Webb's cognitive thinking models; thus it will likely result in boredom and/or apathy (Shabatu, 2018).

Scaffolded learning targets that are written with higher order thinking in mind can assist with the delivery of more intentional lessons to give students opportunities to answer questions about the content. By intentionally scaffolding their instruction, teachers can also provide students with opportunities to discuss or debate the meaningful implications with an authentic real-world problem solving or decision-making context. Research indicates that teachers who purposely and persistently integrate higher order thinking skills and strategies into their instruction can foster the development of critical thinking capabilities in their students while also bolstering their students' self-confidence and open-mindedness (Miri, David, & Uri, 2007).

Work Cited

Anderson, L. W. & Krathwohl, D. R. (Eds.) (2001). *A taxonomy for learning, teaching, and assessing: A revision of Bloom's taxonomy of educational objectives: Complete edition.* New York: Longman.

Armstrong, P. (2019) Bloom's Taxonomy. Retrieved from https://cft.vanderbilt.edu/guides-sub-pages/blooms-taxonomy/

Bloom, B. S. (1956). *Taxonomy of educational objectives, handbook 1: Cognitive domain.* New York: Longman.

Brophy, J. (April 1992). Probing the Subtleties of Subject-Matter Teaching. *Educational Leadership,* 49(7), 5.

Churches, A. (2009) Blooms digital taxonomy: It's not about tools, its using the tools to facilitate learning. www.academia.edu/30868755/Andrew_Churches_-_Blooms_Digital_Taxonomy.pdf

Heick, T. (2019) What is bloom's taxonomy? A definition for teachers. Retrieved from https://www.teachthought.com/learning/what-is-blooms-taxonomy-a-definition-for-teachers/.

McNulty, N. (2017) Blooms digital taxonomy. Retrieved from www.niallmcnulty.com/2017/11/blooms-digital-taxonomy/

Miri, B., David, B. C., & Uri, Z. (2007). Purposely teaching for the promotion of higher-order thinking skills: A case of critical thinking. *Research in Science Education,* 37(4), 353–369. doi: 10.1007/s11165-006-9029-2.

Mississippi state University (2009) *Webb's depth of knowledge guide: Career and technical education definitions.* Retrieved from www.aps.edu/sapr/documents/resources/Webbs_DOK_Guide.pdf

Revised Blooms Taxonomy (2020) Retrieved from www.celt.iastate.edu/teaching/effective-teaching-practices/revised-blooms-taxonomy/

Ritchhart, R. (2002). *Intellectual Character: What it is, why it matters, and how to get it.* San Francisco: Jossey-Bass.

Ritchhart, R., Palmer, P., Church, M., & Tishman, S. (2006) Thinking routines: Establishing patterns of thinking in the classroom. AERA Conference, 2006: Harvard Graduate School of Education.

Roberts, M. J. & Erdos, G. (1993). Strategy selection and metacognition. *Educational Psychology,* 13(3–4), 259–266. doi: 10.1080/0144341930130304.

Shabatu, J. (2018) Using bloom's taxonomy to write effective learning objectives. Retrieved from https://tips.uark.edu/using-blooms-taxonomy/

Shukla, D. & Dungsungnoen, P. (2016). Student's perceived level and teachers' teaching strategies of higher order thinking skills; A study on higher educational institutions in Thailand. *Journal of Education and Practice*, 7(12), 211–219.

Webb, N. (1997). Research monograph number 6: Criteria for alignment of expectations and assessments on mathematics and science education. Retrieved from http://facstaff.wceruw.org/normw/WEBBMonograph6criteria.pdf. 12/5/19

Webb, N. (2002) Depth-of-Knowledge levels for four content areas. Retrieved from http://facstaff.wcer.wisc.edu/normw/All%20content%20areas%20%20DOK%20levels%2032802.pdf. 12/5/19

10 Write Learning Targets for the Standard

 Introduction

All the work and reading you have done in the previous chapters have brought you to this point. Unpacking your standards prior to writing the corresponding learning targets is critical to ensuring that you properly align student learning outcomes to your prescribed standards. The most ideal time to write learning targets for a standard is when you are most familiar with the standard, which is why this is the concluding step in the unpacking process.

Two types of learning targets to focus on integrating into the unpacking process are:

1. the overarching learning target; and
2. the lesson specific learning target.

Both serve a unique instructional purpose that play an important part in scaffolding your instructional delivery. In their book *Scaffolding Science Inquiry Through Lesson Design*, Klentschy and Thompson (2008) identify the relationship between how, in our personal lives, we make goals and set objectives that help us stay on track and monitor our daily progress. They apply this same principal to the classroom and state that knowing what to teach can often be more important than knowing how to teach. There is an inherent risk when one jumps into an instructional unit without first obtaining a clear understanding of the content goals and other learning objectives. Without a strategically scaffolded approach to teaching and learning there is also a risk that important content may be missed because one may not clearly understand how to appropriately build their content lessons to reach the desired learning objectives (pg. 15). Daily learning targets should be designed to gradually increase students' understanding of the prerequisite knowledge and skills needed to prepare them for future lessons (Moss & Brookhart, 2014).

There is a plethora of research that supports the positive impacts of identifying and sharing learning targets with students. Marzano (2003) stated that both student achievement and understating of their content is enhanced when the objectives of a unit are identified and shared. These gains can be enhanced when the learning goals are clearly stated (Moss & Brookhart, 2014; Seidel, Rimmele, & Prenzel, 2005). Klentschy and Thompson (2008) expand on this by telling us that the effectiveness of instruction can be severely undercut when one is not able to state the explicit focus of each lesson in student and teacher-friendly language. When students understand exactly what they're supposed to learn and have exemplars that demonstrate what that learning looks like, they are positioned to more effectively monitor and adjust their work, select effective strategies, and connect current work to prior learning (Black et al., 2004; Moss, Brookhart, & Long, 2011). These findings have been consistent across lower (Higgins, Harris, & Kuehn, 1994) and upper grade levels (Ross & Starling, 2008); and in a variety of subjects (Andrade, Du, & Mycek, 2010; Ross et al., 2002; Ross & Starling, 2008).

Identifying and writing learning targets will make it easier to understand the curriculum and to design your lesson in order to scaffold to the final learning objective(s) for your standard(s). They serve as a starting point for your lesson planning and will help ensure that your instruction targets the intended learning outcomes "understanding the *intended curriculum* is the starting point for all lesson planning ... The careful crafting of what is intended to be taught lays the groundwork for what is actually taught" (Klentschy & Thompson, 2008 pg. 16).

Overarching Learning Target

The first and arguably the easiest type of learning target to write is the overarching learning target. The purpose of the overarching learning target is to bring the desired instructional outcomes for a set of lessons to your students. Although it is important to post your overarching learning target in the classroom, it is not necessarily the tool you will use to drive the focal point of each individual lesson. This learning target focuses on the final learning outcome(s) for an instructional standard(s). Because of this, the overarching learning target can have a high potential of being used incorrectly in the classroom.

Allow me to explain the purpose of an overarching learning target using the analogy of navigation. When you need to get to a specific destination, you enter the name of the establishment or the address of your destination. This final destination would be your overarching learning target.

The navigation system will then direct you through a series of short instructions, such as "continue straight on Franklin Blvd for 6 miles", or "turn left on Main Street." These short pieces of instruction can be likened to your lesson-specific learning targets. Each daily lesson is scaffolded to bring you to your overarching learning target just as the turn-by-turn directions on your GPS bring you to your desired location.

The overarching learning target is used when introducing a new concept or skill that is encompassed in a standard or set of related standards. The concepts and/or skills in this target are too multifaceted to be taught in a single day. You wouldn't write a single learning target and leave it posted on the board for the days or weeks it may take to teach the aligning standard(s), but you could use it as an overarching learning target that would guide you in creating a series of scaffolded lessons to bring your students to the final learning objective(s).

Lesson-Specific Learning Target

Moss and Brookhart (2012) describe daily learning targets as theories of action that connect the essential content to effective instruction and subsequently meaningful learning. They further articulate this theory of action by providing nine action points that accentuate the validity of this statement. The initial theory of action, which I believe to be the most impactful, states "Learning targets are the first principal of meaningful learning and effective instruction" (pg. 12).

Consider the implications of: "Learning targets are the **first**..." not the second or third, but the first, as in the primary driving force behind meaningful learning and effective instruction. Lesson-specific learning targets are the foundation for delivering the type of instruction that is going to result in meaningful and intentional student learning. Moss and Brookhart (2012) imply that that this connection is nothing short of simple logic. "To reach a destination, you need to know exactly where you are headed, plan for the best route to get there, and monitor your progress along the way" (pg.13).

Just as the overarching learning target provides a specific and clear final learning outcome(s) for an instructional standard, the lesson-specific learning target focuses specifically on the instructional objective for that day. The teacher scaffolds the skills students will need in order to meet the learning outcomes of the instructional standard(s). The lesson-specific learning target guides the lesson you are delivering today, and the lesson you are delivering today should clearly bring the students to where they need to be by the end of the lesson set. Moss and Brookhart (2012) state that "Today's lesson should serve a purpose in a longer learning trajectory toward some larger leaning goal" (pg. 12). A learning target is only good for one lesson; it should have a specific purpose and should never be redundant by asking students to do more of the same.

Step One

The first step in writing your desired learning target is to start with the Overarching Learning Target and work backwards from there to complete the lesson-specific learning targets. Begin by referencing the work you just completed in the previous part of the process – Standard Reconstruction. In that section you were able to rephrase, simplify, and clarify a standard in student-friendly language; now you just have to turn it into a learning target. In many instances this will be as simple as adding "I can" in front of the reconstructed standard. Although other times you may find that it is more palatable to break the reconstructed standard(s) into more than one overarching learning target or vice-versa. You may take multiple standards and turn them into a single overarching learning target. As long as the learning goals/objectives accurately capture the learning outcome(s) of the standard(s) and are clear and coherent for you and your students, you are good to go.

> **Work Along**
>
> Reread the reconstructed standard and determine if you can simply add "I can" to the beginning of it or if it will be easier for you and/or your students to conceptualize the standard if you break it into more than one overarching learning target.

 ## Step Two

This is the fun part! Utilizing the overarching learning target(s) from the previous step and your district pacing/curriculum guide, determine how many days you have to teach the content. Then, utilize the number of available instructional days to write daily learning targets that will develop the knowledge and/or skills needed to reach the final learning outcome(s).

> **Work Along**
>
> Determine the number of instructional days available to teach the unpacked standard(s).
>
> - Utilize your district pacing and/or curriculum guide if available.
> - Write learning daily learning targets that break scaffold student learning into manageable instructional chunks that can be scaffolded to bring your students to the final learning objective(s).

 ## Examples

In the examples on the following pages you can see both the overarching learning target and possible lesson-specific learning targets for each of the example standards. I say "possible" because I feel that it is important to stress that even though the learning targets on the following pages can be used as examples, they are not the only *correct* options. There are

Write Learning Targets for the Standard

multiple variations that one could successfully use to guide their daily instruction and student learning.

How you and your team choose to structure your learning targets and the amount of material taught in a single day could easily differ from these examples due to multiple factors. Everything from the allotted number of instructional days, length of the instructional block (45, 60 min, 90 min), and even sequence of the curriculum can impact how you choose to write your learning targets.

In this first example in Figure 10.1, the overarching learning target is captured by taking the reconstructed standard "Demonstrate understanding of a text by asking and answering questions that refer to the text" and adding *I can* to the beginning of it.

Unpacking Your learning Targets
Standard # - __RI3.1__

Standard 1 – Ask and answer questions to demonstrate understanding of a text, referring explicitly to the text as the basis for the answers.

Cut the Fluff: Reread your grade level standard. Condense and summarize the standard (what do the students need to be able to do, and how)

    What - demonstrate understanding of a text

    How - by asking and answering questions that refer explicitly to the text

Standard Reconstruction: Focusing on what your students are supposed to do and how they are supposed to do it write an explanation and/ or paraphrase the standard in your own words.

Demonstrate understanding of a text by asking and answering questions that refer to the text

Learning Targets: Write learning targets for the standard.

    Overarching learning target (reference "Standard Reconstruction")

 I can demonstrate understanding of a text by asking and answering questions that refer to the text

    Lesson specific Learning targets (reference "Cut the Fluff")

Day 1 - I can refer explicitly to the text to answer who, what, when, were, and why questions about the text.

Day 2 - I can demonstrate understanding of a text by identifying key details from different sections *and explain my thinking*.

Day 3 - I can analyze the meaning of a text by answering questions and using evidence from the text to support my thinking.

Day 4 - I can generate meaningful questions about a text and support my thinking by citing the text.

Figure 10.1 RI3.1 Learning Targets

"*I can* demonstrate understanding of a text by asking and answering questions that refer to the text."

This adjustment may not work for every overarching learning target and there may be some multifaceted standards that require two different overarching learning targets.

In order to tackle the daily learning targets for this standard I went back to the Cut the Fluff section and pulled from what the students are supposed to be able to do, which is "demonstrate understanding on a text". I chose to start with a bigger picture here while simultaneously beginning to reinforce key details.

Day 1: Since the standard does not specify which types of questions students should be able to answer about the text, I used this as an instructional opportunity to reinforce some previous skills. I chose to use the first instructional day to help students understand a text by identifying who, what, when, where, and why questions. Because students will be referring explicitly to the text to answer questions, they will need to recall characters, settings, purpose, and other previously instructed text features. Students will also need to recognize and identify these features in the text.

"I can refer explicitly to the text to answer who, what, when, where, and why questions about the text."

This learning target prepares students for in-depth learning outcomes by engaging them in the lower levels of Bloom's Taxonomy and Webb's Depth of Knowledge. This is ideally where an opening lesson or activity should begin as we help students build the foundation needed to take on more challenging learning goals.

- Connections to Bloom's Taxonomy
    - Knowledge – Students will need to recall the who, what, when, where, and why of a text.
    - Comprehension – Students are demonstrating their understating of the text by locating examples of who, what, when, where, and why within a text.
- Connections to Webb's Depth of Knowledge
    - DOK-1 – Students are identifying details from a text to indicate the who, what, when, where, and why.

Write Learning Targets for the Standard

Day 2: Continuing into day two, I have chosen to integrate the identification of key details into the learning target built upon the previous learning goals.

The learning target for day two states:

"I can demonstrate understanding of a text by identifying key details from different sections."

This learning target requires one to broadly demonstrate understanding of a text by citing key details. It utilizes learning from the previous day by having students apply their knowledge and understanding of the text and key details.

The wording of this learning target also showcases how different verbs can be used to the same affect.

For example:

"I can *demonstrate* understanding of a text by *identifying* key details from different sections."

This can also be expressed to achieve the same instructional outcomes by changing the verbs *demonstrate* and *identify*, for instance:

- "I can *show* understanding of a text by *labeling* key details from different sections"
- "I can *illustrate* understanding of a text by *stating* key details from different sections"
- "I can *articulate* my understanding of a text by *recognizing* key details from different sections"

Each verb in the above examples communicates the same learning outcome. Which verb you choose to use is often just a matter of preference.

I'm not trying to muddy the water or confuse anyone by providing a variety of examples. Rather, I am demonstrating that there is not a single correct learning target that you have to use. You and I may write different learning targets to achieve similar learning outcomes as directed by a standard, and that's okay. We can still both be right.

Depending on the level of the of the class or the length of the lesson, you have the option of digging deeper into this standard by adding "… and explain my thinking" to the end of this learning target, for instance: "I can identify key details from different sections of a text *and explain my thinking*". This brings analysis skills into the lesson and provides a good instructional opportunity for students to demonstrate through turn-and-talks or other mediums.

Write Learning Targets for the Standard

- Connections to Bloom's Taxonomy
    - Application – Students are applying their knowledge and comprehension from the previous lesson by identifying, labeling, or stating the key details from a text. This application confirms their knowledge of key details and their comprehension of a text.
    - *Analysis – If "…and explain my thinking" is added to this learning target, students will need to support their sources by breaking down their thought process.

- Connections to Webb's Depth of Knowledge
    - DOK 2 – By using the identified key details students will be able to demonstrate understanding of the text.
    - *DOK 3 – If "…and explain my thinking" is added to this learning target, students must explain how or why they arrived at the answers they did.

Day 3: Having spent two days of instruction on helping students demonstrate their understanding of a text, it may now be time to move them solidly into the "How" section from Cut the Fluff.

"by asking and answering questions that refer explicitly to the text"

Now that students have received instruction on what they need to look for in order to demonstrate understanding of a text, they must also be able to identify the textual evidence that justifies their thinking. Although it is possible to combine the skills of "asking and answering" together, I am opting to separate them to provide a great instructional focus. As such, the learning target for day three is going to focus specifically on answering questions.

"I can analyze the meaning of a text by answering questions and using evidence from the text to support my thinking."

The learning target for day three continues to reinforce the previous targets by scaffolding the learning and the higher order thinking skills from the previous days. To accomplish this, students must examine and analyze their thinking through the evaluative process of supporting their thoughts through textual evidence.

- Connections to Bloom's Taxonomy
    - Analysis – Students must examine the text in order to distinguish its meaning.

Write Learning Targets for the Standard

- ○ Evaluation – Students must explain/justify their analysis of the text by citing the text to support their thinking.

- Connections to Webb's Depth of Knowledge
  - ○ DOK 2 – Students will apply their understanding of the text to answer questions about the text.
  - ○ DOK 3 – Through this learning target students must explain how or why they arrived at the answers they did.

Day 4: The final daily learning target for RI 3.1 has students move from answering questions to asking questions that refer explicitly to the text. Just as in the previous day's learning target, I am again referencing the "How" section from Cut the Fluff.

"by asking and answering questions that refer explicitly to the text"

In order to continue moving students through all the skills embedded in this standard, we must ensure that time is spent giving students the opportunity to ask appropriate questions about a text, and that the questions they ask are supported by textual evidence. As such, the sample learning target for day four focuses specifically on asking questions.

"I can generate meaningful questions about a text and support my thinking by citing the text."

In this learning target, students are asked to demonstrate the two highest levels of Bloom's taxonomy. First, they must synthesize the text in order to formulate meaningful questions. Then, they must evaluate and defend their thinking based on what they read in the text.

- Connections to Bloom's Taxonomy
  - ○ Analysis – Students must examine the text in order to distinguish its meaning.
  - ○ Synthesis – In order to compose meaningful questions, students must be able to categorize the key details and meaning of the text to create thoughts and questions about the text and/or its content.
  - ○ Evaluation – Students must explain/justify their understanding and questions by citing specific parts of the text to support their thinking.

- Connections to Webb's Depth of Knowledge
  - ○ DOK 2 – Students will apply their understanding of the text to answer questions about the text.

Write Learning Targets for the Standard

- DOK 3 – Through this learning target students must explain how or why they arrived at the answers they did.
- DOK 4 – Students are extending their thinking by establishing connections from the text to their prior knowledge to compose meaningful questions. Students may consider question starters such as what could/would happen if…? Why was _____ impacted by…? What if…?

The overarching learning target, in Figure 10.2, was pulled out of a portion of the reconstructed standard.

Unpacking Your learning Targets
Standard # - <u>7G.A.2</u>

Standard 2 - Draw (freehand, with a ruler and protractor, and with technology) geometric shapes with given conditions. Focus on constructing triangles from three measures of angles or sides, noticing when the conditions determine a unique triangle, more than one triangle, or no triangle.

Cut the Fluff: Reread your grade level standard. Condense and summarize the standard (what do the students need to be able to do, and how)

    What - <u>Draw geometric shapes, construct triangles, notice when given conditions determine a unique triangle, more than one triangle, or no triangle.</u>

    How – <u>Free hand, with a ruler, and with technology from three measures of angles or sides</u>

Standard Reconstruction: Focusing on what your students are supposed to do and how they are supposed to do it write an explanation and/ or paraphrase the standard in your own words.

<u>Draw geometric shapes, focusing on triangles and identifying when given conditions determine a unique triangle, more than one triangle, or no triangle. Construct the shapes from three given measures of angles or sides, drawing them free hand, with a ruler, and with technology.</u>

Learning Targets: Write learning targets for the standard.

    Overarching learning target (reference "Standard Reconstruction")

<u>I can draw geometric shapes and identify how given conditions determine a unique triangle, more than one triangle, or no triangle.</u>

    Lesson specific Learning targets (reference "Cut the Fluff")

Day 1 – I can identify a variety of geometric shapes and retell the conditions for a unique triangle.

Day 2 - I can explain how a shape's angles and sides define what type of shape it is and how given conditions can result in either a unique triangle or multiple types of triangles.

Day 3 - I can use the given conditions to draw and correctly identify geometric shapes free hand, with a ruler, and with technology.

Day 4 - I can create the conditions needed to draw various geometric shapes, including unique triangles, and more than one triangle and justify my thinking.

Figure 10.2 7G.A.2 Learning Targets

Write Learning Targets for the Standard

> Draw geometric shapes, focusing on triangles and identifying when given conditions determine a unique triangle, more than one triangle, or no triangle. Construct the shapes from three given measures of angles or sides, drawing them free hand, with a ruler, and with technology.

Unlike the previous example, where we were able to add *I can* to the beginning of the reconstructed standard and keep it in student-friendly language, Standard 7G.A2 is much wordier, so that strategy is probably not in the best interest of the learners.

To write a clear overarching learning target, separate what the students need to know in order to master their overarching learning objective vs what can be given to them through the daily learning targets. This needs to be done without hindering their understanding of the learning outcomes. With this standard, you can reduce the overarching learning target to:

"I can draw geometric shapes and identify how given conditions determine a unique triangle, more than one triangle, or no triangle."

In this example the methodology for how students will draw geometric shapes can be informed through the daily learning targets. It is not a necessary component of the overarching learning target. Inform students of the expectation that they must draw geometric shapes. The multiple ways they will demonstrate this can easily be integrated into the daily learning targets without encumbering the overarching learning target.

As in the previous example, first look at what students are supposed to accomplish in order to appropriately frame our daily learning targets. Referencing the Cut the Fluff section in Figure 10.2, notice you can see that students are supposed to be able to do two things:

1. Draw geometric shapes; and
2. notice when given conditions determine a unique triangle, more than one triangle, or no triangle.

Day 1: Before having students start to draw shapes it is important to begin the instruction for this standard with identifying a variety of different shapes and also differentiating multiple types of triangles. If you skip over this core piece of knowledge affirmation and/or acquisition, then you could run the risk of getting into content that some students may not have the foundation to appropriately grasp. Therefore, it could be a good use of instructional time to ensure that all students have the foundational geometric knowledge to successfully wade into the depths of this standard.

The sample learning target for Day 1 states:

"I can identify a variety of geometric shapes and retell the conditions for a unique triangle."

Not only does this learning target represent a good use of our instructional time to reinforce prior knowledge/learning of the standard, it also begins student learning at the lower levels of Bloom's taxonomy and Webb's Depth of Knowledge.

- Connections to Bloom's Taxonomy
  - Knowledge – There should be geometric shapes that all students can recall from previous knowledge. The teacher may also give students new shapes to identify/recognize.
  - Comprehension – Students can demonstrate their previous knowledge and any newly-acquired knowledge of geometric shapes by identifying said shapes and distinguishing between different types of triangles.

- Connections to Webb's Depth of Knowledge
  - DOK-1 – Students are being asked to demonstrate basic geometric facts (shape identification) in order to prepare them for deeper thinking.

Day 2: Building on knowledge acquisition from the previous day, I wanted students to be able to demonstrate their understanding of geometric shapes on a deeper level than just basic identification. In this sample learning target students must articulate their thinking of how angles and sides determine various shapes while also applying their knowledge of the conditions needed to form a unique triangle.

"I can explain how a shape's angles and sides define what type of shape it is and how given conditions can result in either a unique triangle or multiple types of triangles."

Instructionally this learning target provides the teacher with an opportunity to start with some easier examples using a variety of shapes before moving to having students explain the various conditions for unique triangles.

Write Learning Targets for the Standard

It is also permissible to split this learning target into two pieces in order to make the learning outcomes clearer to students:

"I can explain how a shape's angles and sides define what type of shape it is"

and...

"I can explain how given conditions can result in either a unique triangle or multiple types of triangles"

This is another example of teacher preference, and I'm not going to argue that one is either right or wrong/better or worse. Determine what works better for you and your students to facilitate the desired learning outcomes. At the end of the day, they are both asking students to demonstrate the same things, and neither will differently impact the focus of the instruction or the way in which the content is taught.

- Connections to Bloom's Taxonomy
    - Comprehension – Students must demonstrate understanding of geometrical facts through explanation

- Connections to Webb's Depth of Knowledge
    - DOK 2 – Students are demonstrating both factual and conceptual knowledge of geometric shapes and they are applying their knowledge of angles and sides in order to express understanding though a variety of explanations.

Day 3: When drafting learning targets, it is often useful to think about how you will approach them instructionally. The learning targets leading up to Day 3 focused mostly on knowledge acquisition and checks for comprehension. In Day 3, the sample learning target moves students into higher order thinking skills by asking students to apply the knowledge from the previous lessons in order to complete instructional tasks.

"I can use the given conditions to draw and correctly identify geometric shapes free hand, with a ruler, and with technology."

Reflect

What do you see happening in a classroom where this learning target is the focus of the classroom instruction and student tasks?

Write Learning Targets for the Standard

I imagine students working in one of three stations (drawing either freehand, with a ruler, or on a computer, tablet, or interactive display) using the given conditions to appropriately identify a variety of geometric shapes. Aligning the learning target to student tasks often helps when identifying either the level of Higher Order Thinking and/or Depth of Knowledge.

- Connections to Bloom's Taxonomy
    - Application – students must identify and apply their knowledge of angles and measurements in order to draw various geometric shapes.
    - Analysis – students must analyze the conditions they are given in order to assemble their geometric shapes while also determining the shape they are making. This analysis will be especially important when the given conditions result in either a unique triangle or more than one potential triangle.

- Connections to Webb's Depth of Knowledge
    - DOK 2 – Students must identify and apply their knowledge of angles and measurements in order to accomplish the tasks of correctly drawing various geometric shapes.
    - DOK 3 – Similar to the justification used in the "Analysis" of Bloom's Taxonomy, students must analyze the conditions they are given in order to assemble their geometric shapes, transferring their previously acquired knowledge though both their drawings and the identification of their created shapes. The proper analysis of the given conditions are especially important when the given conditions result in either a unique triangle or more than one potential triangle.

Day 4: The goal of the final sample learning target for 7G.A.2 is to provide students with an opportunity to utilize all the acquired knowledge and skills they have learned up to this point and demonstrate proficiency through self-selected geometric conditions. Utilizing the Day 4 learning target:

"I can create the conditions needed to draw various geometric shapes, including unique triangles and more than one triangle, and justify my thinking."

Write Learning Targets for the Standard

students must demonstrate their understanding of how different conditions (angles/sides) combine to form geometric shapes, including unique triangles, and more than one triangle. Thinking through a few instructional options that teachers could facilitate student learning in order to help them "create the conditions needed...":

1. students could draw and label their shapes by having complete freedom to choose any conditions they want.
2. students could narrate their thoughts and then have a partner attempt to follow their instructions to draw and identify a geometric shape.
3. student could work within a series of predetermined parameters in order to provide appropriate guidance while still allowing for induvial creativity.

As previously discussed, you may find it helpful to align your learning targets to higher order thinking skills by envisioning potential tasks that students could do to demonstrate proficiency of a desired learning outcome. Thinking through the instructional tasks that align to each learning target allows you to easily use a scaffolded approach to teaching and learning.

- Connections to Bloom's Taxonomy
  - Synthesis – In order to create the conditions for the necessary geometric shapes, students must be able to appropriately recognize and assemble the necessary angles and sides.
  - Evaluation – By justifying/explaining the thought process they and used to create necessary conditions for their geometric shapes, students will have to assess their final products through an evaluative method.

- Connections to Webb's Depth of Knowledge
  - DOK 3 – In order to demonstrate proficiency of this learning target, students must utilize their conceptual and procedural understandings of the previous day's learning. The previous learning must then be transferred to the geometric shapes they created in order to explain the geometric shapes they created.

Standard Bio.2.2.1 is an excellent example of why I prefaced this section by saying the learning targets here are "possible" examples and that multiple factors must be taken into consideration when writing them. The length of the instructional block, pacing, and curriculum are all factors that must be considered when writing your learning targets.

1. Does your school operate on a traditional schedule or block schedule?
2. Is Biology one semester or two?
3. Does your pacing guide revisit the standard throughout the year?

All of these situations are going to have huge impacts on how you much time you can dedicate to a standard, and will greatly influence how you write and structure your learning targets.

To highlight the versatility of corresponding learning targets for Bio2.2.1, potential learning targets for 3–8 days of instruction are provided. There are also multiple opportunities for curricular enrichment and extensions through a variety of problem/project-based learning opportunities that a teacher could incorporate as part of a larger unit of study.

The sample learning targets provide three days of instruction with possible extensions in days 2 and 3 for a total of up to eight days. In either scenario the learning targets still demonstrate a scaffolded instructional approach to this standard.

It should come as no surprise that allowing more time will provide additional learning opportunities and in-depth student learning, but I am not advocating for one approach over another for this type of standard. That is for you to decide based on the influencing factors listed above. Rather, I am demonstrating the thought process for breaking down a standard into scaffolded learning goals to align with various instructional time constraints/flexibilities.

In Figure 10.3 the overarching learning target was pulled out of a portion of the reconstructed standard stating: "Infer how human activities may impact the environment paying special attention to population growth, pollution, global warming, burning fossil fuels, habitat deconstruction, and the introduction of non-native species." Instead of adding "I can" to the beginning of the reconstructed standard, you can go back to the "What" section from Cut the Fluff to help with this. The other components of the standard can be captured in each of the daily learning targets. This will ensure that you don't miss any of the dictates for student

Write Learning Targets for the Standard

Unpacking Your learning Targets
Standard # - <u>Bio.2.2.1</u>

Standard 3 – Infer how human activities (including population growth, pollution, global warming, burning of fossil fuels, habitat destruction and introduction of nonnative species) may impact the environment.

Cut the Fluff: Reread your grade level standard. Condense and summarize the standard (what do the students need to be able to do, and how)

    What – <u>Infer how human activities may impact the environment</u>

    How – <u>including population growth, pollution, global warming, burning of fossil fuels, habitat destruction and introduction of nonnative species</u>

Standard Reconstruction: Focusing on what your students are supposed to do and how they are supposed to do it write an explanation and/ or paraphrase the standard in your own words.

<u>Infer how human activities may impact the environment paying special attention to population growth, pollution, global warming, burning fossil fuels, habitat deconstruction, and the introduction of nonnative species.</u>

Learning Targets: Write learning targets for the standard.

    Overarching learning target (reference "Standard Reconstruction")

<u>I can infer how a variety of human activities may impact the environment</u>

    Lesson specific Learning targets (reference "Cut the Fluff")

Day 1 – I can identify and understand the differences between a human caused environmental impact and a natural environmental impacts and cycles

*Day 2 – I can explain the root causes of population growth, pollution, global warming, burning fossil fuels, and habitat deconstruction; identify their environmental impacts and infer why they continue to occur.

*Day 3 – I can identify the how human activities have impacted the environment and make reasonable predictions of their continued long-term effects.

Day 4 – I can research and evaluate possible solutions to decrease or stop the environmental impacts of either population growth, pollution, global warming, burning fossil fuels, habitat deconstruction, or the introduction of nonnative species.

*alternate options provided in the examples

Figure 10.3 Bio.2.2.1 Learning Targets

learning and that neither the overarching learning target nor the daily learning targets are overly cumbersome or too wordy.

In this example "I can" is added to the beginning of the task that we pull from the Cut the Fluff section.

"I can Infer how *a variety* of human activities may impact the environment."

I also chose to add the words "a variety" just to emphasize that the following lessons will cover multiple human activities.

Write Learning Targets for the Standard

Day 1: Since every aspect of this standard revolves around the impact of human activities on the environment, students must be able to identify and determine what constitutes as a human activity and how human activities differ from natural environmental cycles and impacts.

"I can explain the root causes of population growth, pollution, global warming, burning fossil fuels, and habitat deconstruction; identify their environmental impacts and infer why they continue to occur."

Spending instructional time on this target will give students prior knowledge to draw from as the lessons progress through this standard, and allows them to make connections on how human activities can impact natural cycles and/or events (such as climate change, floods, storms, etc.).

- Connections to Bloom's Taxonomy
    - Knowledge – By the end of Day 1, students will need to be able to recall the differences between natural environmental events and cycles and those that are caused or impacted by humans.
    - Comprehension – Students will need to demonstrate their understanding of natural and human-caused environmental impacts. This could be approached through classification, explanations, and/or other methods.

- Connections to Webb's Depth of Knowledge
    - DOK 1 – Students will need to be able to recall details to differentiate between human-caused and natural changes in the environment.
    - DOK 2 – Students will need to demonstrate their understanding of natural and human-caused environmental impacts. This could be approached through classification, explanations, and/or other methods.

Day(s) 2–4*: Building upon the previous day's lesson, students will dig deeper into the impacts of human activities on the environment. Identify and analyze the causality of these activities and the probable impacts of them.

Write Learning Targets for the Standard

"I can explain why human impacts such as population growth, pollution, global warming, burning fossil fuels, habitat deconstruction, and the introduction of non-native species exist and infer why they continue to occur."

This learning target serves as another example of how the length of an instructional block and/or district pacing could easily influence the composure of a learning target. A teacher could justifiably choose to break these learning outcomes into multiple days, separating each of the human activities into different days or by pairing some together. Here are three possible alternatives.

Day 2: I can explain the root causes of population growth and habitat deconstruction, identify their environmental impacts, and infer why they continue to occur.

Day 3: I can explain the root causes of why we burn fossil fuels and other pollutants, identify their environmental impacts, and infer why they continue to occur.

Day 4: I can explain the root causes of global warming and habitat deconstruction, identify their environmental impacts, and infer why they continue to occur.

Whether one chooses to tackle the impacts of human activities all at once or break them apart, their interaction with both Bloom's Taxonomy and Webb's Depth of Knowledge remains the same.

- Connections to Bloom's Taxonomy
    - Application – To demonstrate proficiency of this learning target, students will apply prior and newly-acquired knowledge to explain why we burn fossil fuels, why population growth occurs, etc.
    - Analysis – Students will be inferring why these human activities have continued to occur and identify actual and probable environmental impacts.

- Connections to Webb's Depth of Knowledge
    - DOK 2 – Students will apply their knowledge (prior and newly acquired) to explain why we burn fossil fuels, why population growth occurs, etc.
    - DOK 3 – Students will analyze their knowledge to draw reasonable conclusions of why these human activities have continued to occur and identify actual and probable environmental impacts.

Write Learning Targets for the Standard

Day(s) 3–7*: To demonstrate proficiency of today's learning target, students will need to identify previously discussed human activities and recall their environmental impacts. By taking the instructional tasks a step further, students must also make logical and predictive analyses of potential environmental outcomes if already discussed human activities remain unchecked.

"I can identify how human activities have impacted the environment and make reasonable predictions of their continued long-term effects."

In order to guide student learning, a teacher could choose to facilitate activities that include potential best-case and worst-case scenarios. Students could also work collaboratively on a single human activity (i.e. burning fossil fuels, habitat deconstructions, etc). Or, similar to the previous learning target, students could work through the environmental impacts of the various human activities on different days. Breaking this learning target into multiple days could look something like this:

Day 3/5*: *I can identify how population growth and habitat deconstruction have impacted the environment and make reasonable predictions of their continued long-term effects.*

Day 4/6*: *I can identify how burning fossil fuels and other pollutants have impacted the environment and make reasonable predictions of their continued long-term effects.*

Day 5/7*: *I can identify how global warming and habitat deconstruction have impacted the environment and make reasonable predictions of their continued long-term effects.*

As mentioned at the beginning of this example, this standard also provides opportunities for additional enrichment/extension. Taking into consideration your instructional time frame, you could embrace higher levels of critical thinking by adding "…and evaluate possible solutions" to the learning target, in either its single day or multiday format.

"I can identify how human activities have impacted the environment and make reasonable predictions of their continued long-term effects *and evaluate possible solutions*"

or the multiday approach…

"I can identify how population growth and habitat deconstruction have impacted the environment and make reasonable predictions of their continued long-term effects *and evaluate possible solutions.*"

Write Learning Targets for the Standard

Day 4/6/or 8*: Turning the *evaluation of possible solutions* into its own learning target and/or its problem-based learning project is also a logical possibility. For example:

"I can research and evaluate possible solutions to decrease or stop the environmental impacts of either population growth, pollution, global warming, burning fossil fuels, habitat deconstruction, or the introduction of non-native species."

These options are not meant to confuse the process of writing learning targets or to muddy the proverbial water. Rather they are meant to encourage you to examine your desired learning outcomes as they align to the prescribed standards and your district pacing. The sample learning targets for this standard could be used in any combination to provide instructional outcomes for 3–8 days while utilizing the same overarching learning target.

- Connections to Bloom's Taxonomy
    - Application – In order to *identify how human activities have impacted the environment* students will need to apply their previous learning in a cause and effect method.
    - Analysis – In order to *make reasonable predictions of their continued long-term effects* students will need to begin interpreting the overarching impacts and the interconnectedness of environmental effects.
    - *Synthesis – If ... *and evaluate possible solutions* is added to the learning target, students will need to investigate the cause and effect of a given human activity and its environmental impact(s) and then articulate and/or develop possible solutions to overcome them.
    - Evaluation – After analyzing the overarching impacts students will need to appraise potential trends and outcomes in order to *make reasonable predictions*.

- Connections to Webb's Depth of Knowledge
    - DOK 2 – In order to *identify how human activities have impacted the environment*, students will need to draw conclusions from their previous learning
    - DOK 3 – Students will need to apply strategic thinking to establish cause and effect and interpret potential environmental outcomes.

- o DOK 4 – Students will need to establish connects between current environmental impacts and potential environmental impacts by predicting what could/would happen as a result of given human activities. If ... *and evaluate possible solutions* is added to the learning target, students will further extend their thinking to encompass connections to potential solutions and/or identify their own reasonable solutions.

Conclusion

Throughout each of the examples provided in this chapter, you have been able to draw a continual reference to the previous steps in the unpacking process. This ongoing reference will help to ensure the alignment of your desired learning outcomes to those of the standard(s) you are working with. It is through this process that you will better understand the intended curriculum and strategically approach your daily instruction.

Incorporating and identifying higher order thinking skills, either through Bloom's Taxonomy or Webb's Depth of Knowledge, will assist you in appropriately scaffolding your lessons in order to increase student learning. Providing students with opportunities to think critically is an essential component of equitable instruction that will foster higher levels of student performance (Noguera, 2017). Providing students with sequenced instruction that is aligned to your state standards will help to ensure that students master the objectives that they will eventually be assessed on (Noguera 2017, 2018).

In her book *How It's Being Done: Urgent Lessons from Unexpected Schools*, Karen Chenoweth (2009) relays success stories from multiple schools around the county. She emphasizes the importance of standard-based instruction and how schools that ensure their instruction is aligned with state standards have achieved unexpected growth and performance results. This is exemplified in the recounting of Texas-based Lockhart Junior High School, where the introductory paragraph of the school's success story opens with "It's not rocket science ... you figure out what you need to teach, and then you teach it" (p. 94).

Although the process is not rocket science, it is still a process that properly aligns instruction to assessed standards. In Chenoweth's recounting, this does not mean that one is teaching to the test. Rather, they are teaching the learning objectives being assessed by the state. Lockhart approached this by building a sequence of instruction that promotes student mastery of the objectives indicated in the state standards. First, content departments take the time to study and comprehend their standards (unpacking). Next, they develop a curriculum to match the standards. Then they develop lesson plans and common assessments around those desired learning outcomes.

This isn't to say that day-to-day instruction should be a lockstep process. Just because you allotted a certain number of days to teach a standard and have already written the learning targets and lesson plans doesn't mean they can't be changed. If the formative assessment given at the end of the lesson indicates that the students did not grasp key components of the learning target, you may need to reconstruct the next day's learning target to incorporate opportunities for reteaching. You may even determine that a single multifaceted learning target contained too many learning objectives and should be broken into two targets, each with fewer success criteria. Relying on and responding to student data in a timely manner is a trademark of successful teaching and learning. In situations such as this, a teacher would attend to exactly what the students were missing from the lesson. Was it a primary component of the learning target or a secondary skill? Do they need to understand it before they can move on to the next learning target or can it be incorporated as a review in the next lesson?

Regardless of the learning targets or lesson plans that have already been written, rely on student data in order to guide daily instruction. Learning targets are meant to support and be used with the formative assessment process; often times this means modifying or rewriting learning targets and/or lesson plans. Even when it causes more work, strategically responding to student data in a timely manner separates those who chose to simply cover their content vs those who teach with a focus on student learning.

Work Cited

Andrade, H. L., Du, Y., & Mycek, K. (2010). Rubric-referenced self-assessment and middle school students' writing. *Assessment in Education*, 17(2), 199–214.

Black, P., Harrison, C., Lee, C., Marshall, B., & William, D. (2004). Working inside the black box: Assessment for learning in the classroom. *Phi Delta Kappan*, 86(1), 9–21.

Chenoweth, K. (2009). *How It's being done: Academic success in unexpected schools.* Cambridge, MA: Harvard Education Press.

Heick, T. (2019) What is bloom's taxonomy? A definition for teachers. Retrieved from www.teachthought.com/learning/what-is-blooms-taxonomy-a-definition-for-teachers/

Higgins, K. M., Harris, N. A., & Kuehn, L. L. (1994). Placing assessment into the hands of young children: A study of student-generated criteria and self-assessment. *Educational Assessment,* 2(4), 309–324.

Klentschy, M. & Thompson, L. (2008). *Scaffolding science inquiry.* Portsmoth, NH: Heineman.

Marzano, R. (2003). *What works in schools: Translating research into action.* Alexandria, VA: ASCD.

Moss, C. M. & Brookhart, S. M. (2012). *Learning targets: Helping students aim for understanding in today's.* Alexandria, VA: ASCD.

Moss, C. M. & Brookhart, S. M. (2014). Learning targets on parade. *Educational Leadership,* 72(2), 28–33.

Moss, C. M., Brookhart, S. M., & Long, B. A. (2011). Knowing your learning target. *Educational Leadership,* 68(6), 66–69.

Noguera, P. (2017). *Taking deeper learning to scale.* Palo Alt, CA: Learning Policy Institute.

Noguera, P. (2018) Deeper learning: An essential component of equity. Learning Policy Institute, retrieved from https://learningpolicyinstitute.org/blog/deeper-learning-essential-component-equity

Ross, J. A., Hogaboam-Gray, A., & Rolheiser, C. (2002). Student self-evaluation in grade 5–6 mathematics: Effects on problem-solving achievement. *Educational Assessment,* 8, 43–58.

Ross, J. A. & Starling, M. (2008). Self-assessment in a technology-supported environment: The case of grade 9 geography. *Assessment in Education,* 15(2), 183–199.

Seidel, T., Rimmele, R., & Prenzel, M. (2005). Clarity and coherence of lesson goals as a scaffold for student learning. *Learning and Instruction,* 15, 539–556.

11 Assessing Your Learning Targets

Introduction

Imagine – you've done the work of unpacking your standard(s) and you're feeling confident that you understand exactly what your students need to learn. Based off that knowledge and your understanding of the content, you have written learning targets that correspond to the standard(s) you are about to teach. But you're still questioning, "Did I do it right?" "Will my learning targets really impact student learning?" After all, if using learning targets fosters the most effective teaching and the most meaningful student learning (Moss & Brookhart, 2012), then you want to ensure that the learning targets we are using are up to the task.

Or perhaps you are a leader at a school that has struggled to consistently raise student performance and provide equitable instruction to all students and in an effort to improve the focus and quality of the core instruction at your school, you assist teachers with writing their learning targets and require them to be posted and utilized. However, you know that simply having learning targets posted in a classroom will not accomplish anything if they are not written and used properly. It takes time and ongoing attention to improve school-wide instructional practices.

Whether you are in a leadership role and are appraising learning targets in multiple classrooms or writing them for your own use, it is important that they are properly written and effectively used. Figure 11.1 below identifies six items that will assist you with this task and ensure that you'll get the intended benefits from your learning targets.

Assessing Your Learning Targets

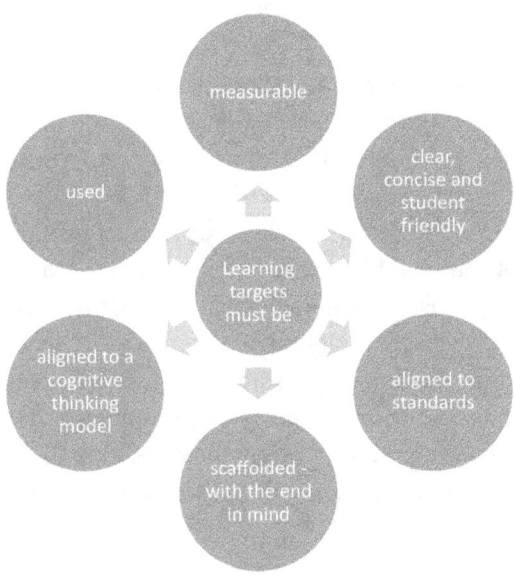

Figure 11.1 Traits of High-Quality Learning Targets

Measurable

All learning targets must include at least one verb that will result in a measurable action, task, or product. One of the intentions of a learning target is to guide daily teaching and learning, but if the intended outcome of the learning target cannot be measured then there is no way to determine if the intended learning actually happened. When you deliberately integrate verbs into your learning targets, you bilaterally work to formulate actions, tasks, and/or products students must complete or demonstrate in order to show mastery of the desired learning target. Examples of appropriate verbs to include are found throughout all versions of Bloom's Taxonomy and Webb's Depth of Knowledge (refer back to Chapter 9 for additional details and examples).

When writing your learning targets, be intentional and consider:

"What learning outcome(s) must my students demonstrate to show that they have achieved the desired learning outcome for today's lesson?"

Then reflect …

"Will demonstrating mastery of this learning target result in the intended learning outcome(s)?"

By first identifying the learning outcome(s) you want students to achieve and then ensuring that the desired outcome(s) is/are clearly connected to your learning target, you can confirm your learning target will, at the very least, align to its intended purpose.

Intentionally utilizing measurable verbs necessitates the creation and/or utilization of measurable tasks. The creation and/or utilization of measurable student tasks helps facilitate classroom instruction that will prepare students for the completion of such tasks. A learning target that does not contain at least one measurable action will foster instructional practices and tasks that lack a clear learning outcome. The lack of clear learning outcomes encumbers student learning and increases the likelihood that classroom instruction will fail to meet its intended purpose.

Clear, Concise, and Student-Friendly

Be clear. What is it that the students should be able to do by the end of the lesson? Don't make your learning targets out to be a game of Pictionary or hide-and-seek. Explicitly state what your students are supposed to be able to do by the end of the class and kick any potential ambiguity to the wayside.

Be concise. A learning target is commonly a single statement, such as "I can identify _____ and describe how it _____." Even though it is permissible to utilize multiple sentences for your daily learning targets, try and be as efficient as possible and remove any unnecessary words. There is no need to fluff up a learning target; unnecessary words dilute the effectiveness of your learning target and confuse your students.

Students learn better when they understand their learning goals (Marzano, 2000; Reeves, 2010). Therefore, the language needs to be student-friendly. Keep it grade-level appropriate and include required academic vocabulary. Keep the language accessible to the students, but don't dumb it down. It is important to remember that learning targets are just as important for the students as they are for the teacher.

There are many classroom strategies that can support learning and a student's ability to digest information and master the skills taught within a lesson. Novice learners may not have the background experiences and knowledge required to integrate relevant information or strategically process new concepts. When overloaded with new information, students may not be able to identify what information to prioritize and what information to set aside for later. When this happens, a student can feel overwhelmed and their ability to learn can be jeopardized. For this reason, it is paramount that intended learning goals are clarified and that long-term goals are clearly defined and broken down into short-term, manageable chunks (Posey, 2019).

Aligned to Standards

It should go without saying that your learning targets should align with your standards. However, it is not wise to just assume this is happening. Teachers must work toward alignment; school leaders must regularly monitor and support this work. Your content standards provide a roadmap of instructional outcomes. When they are thoroughly integrated into the planning process, the trade-off may be that some teachers will need to self their long-treasured enhancement units so that students will get a more coherent education (Chenoweth, 2009).

Karen Chenoweth (2009) relays the story of a high school that began its improvement process by identifying requirements per state standards and then mapping their curriculum and instructions from those requirements to ensure that students learn that material (pp. 53–61). There is also a story of a Junior High School that figured out they could achieve amazing results by teaching what students would be assessed on by the state. They don't teach the test; they teach the standards and objectives that students are responsible for demonstrating competency on at the end of the year. Throughout the year, they use school-based common assessment data to figure out the academic needs of their students and then they respond to those needs, always ensuring that they are teaching to the standards (94–101).

Chenoweth (2009) states that all schools that achieve high performance and improvement share a common thread. First, teachers begin with state standards. Then, they think deeply about what their students need to learn and how to make sure they have learned it (p. 216).

When properly used, learning targets can have multiple benefits. They enable teachers to plan and implement effective instruction and they assist educators to accurately respond to student learning, and raise student performance (Moss & Brookhart, 2009, 2012). However, these results will not be realized if there is a misalignment between the leaning objective(s) prescribed by a standard and the learning targets that are supposed to be supporting it. No matter how fantastic the classroom instruction is or how well students perform on their given tasks and assignments, their academic successes in the classroom will fail to translate to increased performance results at the end of the course because they have not learned what the state is going to assess them on.

Daily learning targets and classroom instruction aligned with assessed standards are essential foundational components of school growth. We can't teach students one thing, assess them on something else, and hold the expectation that they will perform well; it simply doesn't make any sense.

Scaffold – With the End in Mind

When you are scaffolding a single lesson or an entire unit, you must begin with the end in mind. By first identifying where you are going, you can better determine how to get there. Essentially, you are working backwards. As Wiggins and McTighe (1998, 2000) articulate their theory of backward design, the idea is that you remain focused on the desired learning outcome(s) and the evidence needed to support the attainment of stated outcomes, instead of losing focus or shifting outcomes to fit preferred activities and/or lessons. The teacher intentionally plans and develops their instruction around the desired learning outcome(s). It is for this reason that the sequence of the unpacking process starts with unpacking standard(s); then write an overarching learning target; then write the lesson-specific learning targets. These three steps happen before you even start planning lessons or activities and help keep your instructional planning focused on the student learning goals while appropriately scaffolding the daily learning goals.

Once you have identified the overarching learning target, identify the knowledge and skills that students must master in order to meet all the learning objectives in the overarching learning target. You can reference

Assessing Your Learning Targets

the Cut the Fluff section from the unpacking document if you are unsure how to get started. From there, begin writing learning targets that address each aspect of the identified learning outcomes. Use your content knowledge to write learning objectives in the order required for students to gain the skills and knowledge needed to progress from mastery of each part to mastery of the whole.

Aligned to a Cognitive Thinking Model

Each learning target needs to clearly corelate to at least one of the levels in a cognitive thinking model, such as Bloom's Taxonomy or Webb's Depth of Knowledge. This correlation should not occur "after-the-fact" or be something that you check for after you have written your learning targets. The process of integrating higher order thinking skills to help build high quality learning targets is most effective when you are intentional about including higher order thinking skills throughout your lessons.

Although learning can happen at any level of Bloom's taxonomy (Anderson & Krathwohl, 2001; Churches, 2009; Shabatu, 2018), it is important to design your learning targets to specifically align to a cognitive thinking model in a scaffolded manner. Begin first with the lower levels of your preferred cognitive model and then progress though the higher order thinking skills. This is no different than planning your lessons around higher order thinking skills where you may assign knowledge and comprehension to the first segment, application and analysis to the second segment, and synthesis and evaluation to the third segment (Gershon, 2013). Assign your first learning targets to the lower levels of the cognitive hierarchy and build your way up to the higher levels by the end of the lesson set. This is a fluid process in which you move between steps based on student needs. For example: if students seem confused during lesson 3 or 4, informally check for understanding and re-teach as necessary before proceeding. The example in Figure 11.2 provides a visual representation of this scaffolding using Boom's Revised taxonomy.

Scaffolding is a key feature of effective teaching and is instrumental in fostering student learning (Vygotsky, 1978; McLeod, 2019). It enables students to achieve learning objectives that would not normally be

Assessing Your Learning Targets

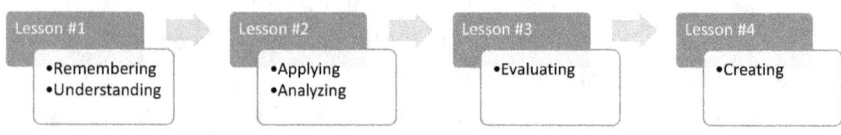

Figure 11.2 Scaffolding Higher Order Thinking Skills into a Lesson Set

obtainable (Wood, Bruner, & Ross, 1976) and can produce immediate leaning gains while also developing independent problem-solving skills (McLeod, 2019). Focusing these efforts, a teacher should be able to clearly delineate what constitutes essential knowledge, understanding, and skills within a content area, unit, and lesson (Sousa & Tomlinson, 2011). This knowledge is used when scaffolding cognitive thinking skills to design a lesson set.

Double check the actionable verbs in your learning targets to ensure that they properly align with the level of learning you are targeting. For example, if you are starting a new lesson set, target the lower levels of cognitive learning. Use words such as define, describe, give examples, and indicate. In later lessons, utilize questioning and activities that derive from verbs such as justify, support, predict, compose, and create.

They Must Be Used

At some point, most of us have been guilty of complying with directives simply because we knew we had to, but never modified our practice as a result of it (Think differentiated instruction, word walls, learning maps, PLCs, and even learning targets). These resources and strategies are meant to improve teaching and learning, but none of them make a bit of difference if they are posted on the wall but never used or are only integrated into a lesson when an administrator walks in.

If you have gone through all the effort of unpacking you learning targets but don't use them, you can't expect to get any noticeable results from your effort. This is the difference between doing something simply for compliance's sake versus integrating it into daily practice.

You may be inclined to ask, "How does one actually use a learning target to improve instruction?" The answer to this question is multi-layered. Assuming you have followed all the other steps in this process, and you have unpacked your standard(s) and written appropriately scaffolded learning targets, you must first allow them to guide your lesson planning. This will likely mean that many of your previous lessons will not align to the learning objectives you are trying to accomplish. It also means that you will have to plan new tasks and activities to help your students achieve these goals. This doesn't mean that you won't be able to reuse or modify some of the activities you have previously created, but it should not be your knee-jerk reaction.

Second, you must post your daily learning target somewhere that is highly visible. If you stick it in the back of the room, your students will assume it is unimportant because it is not visible. Place your learning targets in their line of sight and ensure that they are readable no matter where they are in the classroom. Don't make the mistake of only putting your daily target on the first slide of a Power Point presentation and then clicking away from it so that it is never seen again.

If you post your daily learning target somewhere on the main board, then consider posting the overarching learning target on a side wall, or somewhere else up front. After each lesson, place the daily learning target underneath it and leave it there throughout the lesson set. Each day add the new the learning target. When you do this, students will be able to see the progression of their learning and they will always be reminded of the previous lessons. As a student, just think how many times you used to read the same classroom posters over and over. Give them something to look at that will remind them of their previous learning.

Third, cite your learning targets throughout the lesson. If you are beginning a new lesson, be sure to expose students to the overarching learning target. Then every day, introduce the daily learning target to your class, reference it throughout the lesson and conclude the lesson by revisiting it. A quick informal evaluation at this point, or the opportunity for students to ask clarifying questions, will show the teacher and students whether the desired learning goals have been achieved.

To facilitate your desired learning outcomes, each step of the teaching and learning process needs to be absolutely clear for both teacher and students (Sousa & Tomlinson, 2011).

Conclusion

Writing high quality learning targets takes practice. The process is not inherently difficult, but if the concept is new to you, it can take a little bit of time to get used to. If you are unsure how to proceed or it is too time consuming, don't let it dissuade you from integrating a truly powerful teaching and learning tool into your repertoire. The more learning targets you write, the easier the process will become. You will learn the work by doing the work (Dufour et al., 2010).

Work Cited

Ainsworth, L. (2010). *Rigorous curriculum design: How to create curricular units that align standards, instruction, and assessment.* Englewood, CO: The Leadership and Learning Center.

Anderson, L. W. & Krathwohl, D. R. (Eds.) (2001). *A taxonomy for learning, teaching, and assessing: A revision of Bloom's taxonomy of educational objectives: Complete edition.* New York: Longman.

Bambrick-Santoyo, P. (2016). *Get better faster: A 90 day plan for coaching new teachers.* San Francisco, CA: Jossey-Bass.

Chenoweth, K. (2009). *How it's being done: Academic success in unexpected schools.* Cambridge, MA: Harvard Education Press.

Churches, A. (2009) Blooms digital taxonomy: It's not about tools, its using the tools to facilitate learning. www.academia.edu/30868755/Andrew_Churches_-_Blooms_Digital_Taxonomy.pdf

Dufour, R., Dufour, B., Eaker, R., & Many, T. (2010). *Learning by doing: A Handbook for professional learning communities at work.* Bloomington, IN: Solution Tree Press.

Fixsen, D. L., Naoom, S. F., Blase, K. A., Friedman, R. M., & Wallace, F. 2005. Tampa, FL: University of South Florida, Louis de la Parte Florida Mental Health Institute, The National Implementation Research Network.

Gershon, M. (2013) How to use blooms taxonomy in the classroom: Practical ideas and strategies to help put the taxonomy of educational objectives to work in your classroom. Retrieved from https://academi

camentoring.com/wp-content/uploads/2017/01/How-to-use-Blooms-Taxonomy-in-the-classroom.pdf

Goodwin, B. & Ross Hubbell, E. (2013). *The 12 touchstones of good teaching: A checklist for staying focused everyday*. Alexandria, VA: ASCD.

Grossman, D. (2016) 4 main problems that come with poor communication. Retrieved from www.yourthoughtpartner.com/blog/4-main-problems-that-come-with-poor-communication

Herschell, A. D., Kolko, D. J., Baumann, B. L., & Davis, A. C. (2010). The role of therapist training in the implementation of psychosocial treatments: A review and critique with recommendations. *Clinical Psychology Review*, 30(4), 448–466. 10.

Joyce, B. R. & Showers, B. (2002). *Designing training and peer coaching: Our needs for learning*. VA, USA: ASCD.

Kanter, R. M. (2012) Harvard Business Review https://hbr.org/2012/09/ten-reasons-people-resist-chang

Leithwood, K., Seahorse Louis, K., Anderson, S., & Wahlstrom, K. (2004) How leadership influences student learning. Retrieved from www.wallacefoundation.org/knowledge-center/Documents/How-Leadership-Influences-Student-Learning.pdf

Lyon, A. (2012) Implementation science and practice in the education sector. Retrieved from https://education.uw.edu/sites/default/files/Implementation%20Science%20Issue%20Brief%20072617.pdf

Marzano, R. J. (2000). *A new era of school reform: Going where the research takes us*. Aurora, CO: Mid-continent Research for Education and Learning.

McLeod, S. A. (2019). Zone of proximal development. Retrieved from www.simplypsychology.org/Zone-of-Proximal-Development.html

Moss, C. M. & Brookhart, S. M. (2009). *Advancing formative assessment in every classroom: A guide for instructional leaders*. Alexandria, VA: ASCD.

Moss, C. M. & Brookhart, S. M. (2012). *Learning targets: Helping students aim for understanding in today's*. Alexandria, VA: ASCD.

Posey, A. (2019). *Engage the brain: How to design for learning that taps into the power of emotion*. Alexandria, VA: ASCD.

Reeves, D. B. (2010) Standards, assessment, & accountability: Real questions from educators with real answers from Douglass B. Reeves, Ph.D. Englewood, CO: The Leadership and Learning Center.

Shabatu, J. (2018) Using bloom's taxonomy to write effective learning objectives. Retrieved from https://tips.uark.edu/using-blooms-taxonomy/

Sousa, D. A. & Tomlinson, C. A. (2011). *Differentiation and the brain: How neuroscience supports the learner-friendly classroom.* Bloomington, IN: Solution Tree Press.

Vygotsky, L. S. (1978). *Mind in society: The development of higher psychological processes.* Cambridge, MA: Harvard University Press.

Wiggins, G. & McTighe, J. (1998). *Understanding by design.* Alexandria, VA: ASCD.

Wiggins, G. & McTighe, J. (2000). *Understanding by design expanded 2nd edition.* Alexandria, VA: ASCD.

Wood, D., Bruner, J., & Ross, G. (1976). The role of tutoring in problem solving. *Journal of Child Psychology and Child Psychiatry,* 17, 89–100.

12 | Getting Started

Introduction

The focus of this book has largely dealt with the process of unpacking standards and writing learning targets. Understanding how to do this work is of critical importance, but simply understanding the work isn't going to net you any results or help create high quality learning opportunities for all students. Instead, it is the willingness and dedication to consistently implement the work, either in your school or classroom, that will pay the dividends of your time and effort and provide your students with more equitable learning opportunities.

Instructional standards are a great resource to ensure universally rigorous and concise grade-to-grade learning expectations (Ainsworth, 2010), if educators take the time to familiarize themselves with them through an unpacking process.

Learning targets can help teachers align their instructions to their intended instructional outcomes (Moss Brookhart, 2012) and the extent to which a school clearly articulates and monitors curriculum ensures its alignment to any high-stake is the number one predictor of student achievement (Goodwin & Ross Hubble 2013; Marzano, 2000). However, if the learning targets are either misaligned to the standards that are being assessed or not being used as intended, then these benefits and growth opportunities will not be realized. When written and used properly, learning targets can be a great instructional resource. However, no matter how well-written they are, if you don't use them, they are essentially worthless.

Communicate Purpose and Action Steps

I find it highly improbable that an educational leader would take the time to read a book such as this, endeavor to go through the processes, and teach others to do the same, while internalizing a desire to sabotage their work and the outcomes of their students. I also find it highly unlikely that a well-intentioned classroom teacher would only choose to feign compliance of such a powerful and easy-to-use instructional resource in lieu of proper implementation.

I am much more inclined to believe that faulty implementation is more commonly caused by a misunderstanding of operational protocols or from a failure to appropriately communicate the purpose of an initiative; essentially answering "why" someone should embrace this and providing adequate professional development and support for "how" it is supposed to be used in the classroom.

Purpose

When it comes to school improvement the ability to clearly communicate and set directions has been suggested to account for the largest proportion of a leader's impact (Leithwood, Louis, Anderson, & Wahlstrom, 2004). Whether you are the Principal of a school or a classroom teacher you are still a leader, and leadership is second only to classroom instruction among all school-related factors that contribute to student learning. This is because great leaders have the ability to leverage the tools and assets at their disposal to achieve desired outcomes, their high expectations align to lofty but attainable goals, and their intent is clearly communicated so that it is understood by all (Leithwood, Louis, Anderson, & Wahlstrom, 2004).

A school or classroom leader who is either implementing learning targets for the first time, or just trying to establish more consistency across the entire building or a single classroom, needs to be sure to provide clear expectations to their staff and/or students while also providing them with the appropriate supports to reach and hopefully exceed expectations.

Perpetuating the faulty implementation of evidence-based programs and practices can be aggravated by an insufficient clarity and/or demonstration of purpose. When the people responsible for carrying out an initiative at the ground level are not provided with a clear purpose and rationale of the value of the work, it can leave them to question why they are spending their time on it in the first place.

This lack of understanding and purpose may then logically lead to pushback, intentional evasion of the new program, and outwardly feigning compliance in lieu of actual implementation. These behaviors are more likely to occur when people don't understand the value or purpose of what they are being asked to do. Although leaders don't intentionally withhold critical information, they do often make the mistake of assuming that others know what they know. They may believe that they have appropriately communicated their purpose or intent, but disseminating a message properly means that the message resonates with the target audience and is understood in a way that will motivate the listener into action (Grossman, 2016).

In situations such as this, either the school or district leadership may be very excited about a new initiative. They have probably been to numerous trainings, read the relevant literature, and seen the positive impacts the initiative can have. It is then with the best of intent that they bring initiative X to their school or district, but in their excitement to provide better opportunities to the students, they fail to provide those that are responsible for implementing the initiative with similar exposure or PD. People then push back against the initiative because it is dropped on them so suddenly that they don't have time to digest the information or get used to the idea and the changes it will bring about (Kanter, 2012). This can, unfortunately, leave teachers scratching their heads and thinking to themselves "fake it till we make it" or "this too shall pass".

It should go without saying that the role you have within a school or district will largely dictate your target audience and that your communications should be specific to your target audience. This targeted distribution of information and materials is what implementation science refers to as "helping it happen," but simply disseminating information is not enough to change professional behavior. Rather it is the deliberate and effective integration of evidence-based programs and practices in specific settings that will gain the desired change.

Successful communication of new expectations, information, and materials cannot be done through a 15-minute block of time at a faculty meeting that is wedged between policy updates and data reports. One must provide meaningful professional development that models your expectations, clearly aligns to the goals and expectations you have set and is then followed up with individualized support (Leithwood, Louis, Anderson, & Wahlstrom, 2004).

Action Steps

The school leader may know what they want the staff or team to do, but they may not provide clear directions and training for how to do it. Or an initiative may start out strong, but ongoing oversite and support isn't provided, therefore allowing it to fall through the cracks.

It is important to recognize that in most cases, full implementation is a long process, sometimes taking 2–3 years or more (Lyons, 2012; Fixsen, Naoom, & Friedman, 2005). This is important to know because most leaders use evaluation data to assess the effectiveness of new strategies. Unfortunately, many new initiatives and other research-based approaches are discarded before credible data can be collected.

Other initiatives are left in place for years without the necessary professional development to ensure a successful launch and/or support to keep up with individual implementation needs or staff turnover. One of the most supported implementation science findings in the last 15–20 years is that one-time, "train and hope" professional development models are largely ineffective for producing lasting professional behavior change (Lyon 2012, Herchell et al. 2010, Joyce & Showers 2002). No matter how long or intensive a training, the content is extremely unlikely to be used effectively in practice without post-training supports. For example, even trainings that last a week or more will be ineffective unless they are paired with supports like ongoing, targeted consultation or coaching (Lyons, 2012).

The implementation of any evidence-based program or practice occurs over time or through a variety of phases and opportunities for follow up and feedback (Lyons, 2012). In addition to clear rationale, and opportunities to learn the process, staff should also be provided with action steps that are realistic to achieve but also challenging and meaningful. In his book *Get Better Faster*, Paul Bambrick-Santoyo tells us that action steps should be granular in nature, meaning that they should not be broad or murky suggestions such as "use the learning targets in your lesson," or "let students know your expectations." Instead, provide feedback in precise bite-sized action steps that can be implemented right away such as "Tomorrow, I want you to begin your lesson by introducing the learning target to your students, and then facilitate a discussion of what it means," or "Provide your students with work samples that demonstrate mastery of the learning target and samples that do not, so they can have a comparison for their own work."

If you want to make sure that the implementation of learning targets, or any other initiative, is successful at either a team, school, or district level, you must ensure that appropriate PD and follow up supports are provided on an ongoing basis.

Helpful Tips

Exit Tickets

Many teachers incorporate checks for understanding or small formative assessments throughout their lessons. They do this to make sure their students are learning the appropriate information so they can either move on to the next part, take time as a whole class to review the information that was just given, or determine groups that need extra assistance. Constantly assessing one's instruction while teaching can allow teachers to identify and target potential learning difficulties before the students find themselves missing key information or concepts that can make it difficult for them to learn additional scaffolded information from that point forward.

Compiling these smaller mid-lesson checks for understanding into a final exit ticket or formative assessment can provide both the teacher and student with evidence that the desired learning outcome(s) occurred. I am not advocating that you abandon your smaller mid-lesson check for understanding, as that would be counterintuitive. However, since the learning outcome(s) were made clear at the beginning of the lesson, thanks to the learning target there should be a short check for understanding at the end of the lesson. This will help guide the classroom instruction or targeted learning time at the next available opportunity.

Exit tickets should be short, i.e. a couple of questions, and should take no more than five minutes, if possible. It is also important that the teacher does not help or support the students with the exit ticket, unless it is simply a matter of providing clarity of directions. Helping students with this work will only hinder their learning, and reaffirm low learning expectations, while also making the student work irrelevant for its intended purpose: acquisition of the intended learning objective(s).

Remember that exit tickets are not a tool to "get," "catch," or "surprise" your students with new or different material. It is an opportunity for both the teacher and the student(s) to affirm their leaning and make connections to areas they may need more help on. Also, if you find it difficult to identify or create resources to use in this manner, then it is likely that your learning target is either too broad or lacks a specific learning outcome.

Leverage Resources

Don't be an island. You don't have to do this work all by yourself. In fact, I would never recommend it. Whether you have a team that you can partner with or a vertical alignment partner that you can coordinate with, find others to do the work with and bounce thoughts and ideas off them.

Ideally, if you have a team to work with, you would all start with a standard or two and work through them together. Doing this will help to ensure that everyone understands the process and is on the same page. Then partner up and give each group a few standards. You may find that your team will be able to get though a significant number of the priority standards in just a few hours and it is not uncommon to be able to complete an academic quarter in just a few hours, assuming you have three or more groups working at the same time.

It is not essential that every person on the team unpacks every standard, but it is essential that everyone reviews them and provides feedback, especially when it comes to the learning targets.

Parents and guardians can also be an underutilized resource because we often don't know what to share or we are hesitant to share or ask too much. This can be due to a fear of overloading parents with too much information or from apprehension that the completion of a task will go undone, resulting in a portion of the students being left behind or receiving poor marks. These are legitimate concerns that are common across schools regardless of grade level and socioeconomic spectrums.

However, many schools already have refined communication systems in place, either in the form of weekly newsletters or constantly updated websites. These communication methods can serve as the perfect vehicle for informing parents and/or caregivers about what their students are learning, and also can provide an outlet for a teacher or team to suggest opportunities or conversation starters that can be used at home to encourage learning. Enriching your classroom instruction using a home-to-school connection doesn't always need to take place in the form of asking students to practice their number facts or study vocabulary words, as Moss and Brookhart (2012) point out:

> you can help your child learn more about the economics of our community by discussing local businesses with your child. Help your child think about what local businesses and service providers make and purchase. Point out all the people your child knows and interacts with who have jobs in our local businesses, organizations, industries, public institutions, and agencies.

Consider sharing your daily learning targets with your families, or at least the overarching learning targets, and provide a few strategies, activities, or conversation starters that families can do at home to promote the learning objectives in the classroom.

Conclusion

In the beginning of this book I acknowledged that educators already have a lot on their plate and that we really don't have the time for just *one more thing*. Perhaps you're thinking "man, you have no idea," but believe me when I tell you I get it, I've been in your shoes, and I'm still in your shoes. You work hard to provide the best opportunities for your students so that they can be successful in both school and in life, and you want them to acquire the skills they need that will guarantee their success. This is what we all want for our students.

The knowledge and skills they need to be successful are already laid out in the academic standards. The standards intentionally build on each other year-to-year, allowing students time to master each concept in incremental portions. Choosing not to teach the standards is choosing to set your students up for failure and is a great way to hand them to the next teacher unprepared and encourage unequitable practices.

Set high expectations for both yourself as a teacher, and your students. Do not use, and do not allow others to use excuses to justify not teaching grade level content, such as "my kids didn't get what they needed at home", "they have such hard home lives", or "our kids aren't like the ones at other schools". This deficit thinking will only succeed in continuing the cycle that we are trying to break.

Take the time to unpack and understand your standards, and then scaffold your learning targets to provide adequate foundational knowledge and skills that will allow all of your students to successfully interact with the curriculum while supporting and enriching them no matter where they are academically.

Build your instructional strategies and pedagogy on a solid foundation that will foster continued growth and success by taking the time to unpack your learning targets.

For Product Safety Concerns and Information please contact our EU
representative GPSR@taylorandfrancis.com
Taylor & Francis Verlag GmbH, Kaufingerstraße 24, 80331 München, Germany

www.ingramcontent.com/pod-product-compliance
Lightning Source LLC
Chambersburg PA
CBHW051528230426
43668CB00012B/1780